Many Ma

Moving from despair and darkness to ...,
one Light; it shines in you. Learn to unveil it by "looking up and
within."

Suhail Mirza

Acclaimed mystical writer and founder of Spiritual Solutions

Dec '19

To Olivia (Livy)

Such a fantastic time meeting you at Caroline's in the summer. This is the book that explains my journey from darkness to light.

Suheil /

Copyright © Suhail Mirza 2018

All rights reserved. No part of this publication may be reproduced, stored in a retrieval system, or transmitted in any form or by any means, electronic, mechanical, photocopy, recording or otherwise, without prior written permission of the copyright owner. Nor can it be circulated in any form of binding or cover other than that in which it is published and without similar condition including this condition being imposed on a subsequent purchaser.

British Library Cataloguing Publication Data.
A catalogue record for this book is available from the British Library.

ISBN: 978-0-244-07606-1

Published by One Light Publishing

Book Design by Josh Trim

PRAISE FOR THE SPIRITUAL WRITING OF *Suhail Mirza*

Suhail is a refreshing and wise spiritual writer and voice much like Rumi or Hafiz. His writings not only teach, they support and expand consciousness, with a beautiful, poetic flow.
Suhail's exceptional scholarly background and words leave my heart more open and full to gain greater understanding of the Divine."
- **Alexandra Sofia, Relationship Strategist, California, USA**

"Suhail Mirza is one of my spiritual heroes. He inspires me with his generosity, the breadth of his knowledge, his compassion for others and his humility and his sincerity. We do well to listen to what he has to say."
Mark Muesse, Professor of Religious Studies and Philosophy, Rhodes College, Memphis, Tennessee, USA.

"Only a select few have the great gift of reaching the inner worlds of others and light them up. One of those beings is Suhail Mirza, whose writing achieves just such a rare alchemy.."
Rafael Ponce Anguiano, Lamar Universidad, Mexico.

" I love that I have in Suhail's platforms another place of refuge. A place where I can go for comfort and reflection. Suhail most definitely encourages readers and followers to truly go within to examine their consciousness. This can be uncomfortable, but most certainly that is where

my spiritual journey, enlightenment and awakening begins."
Wyn Duraes, Sussex, UK.

"Suhail's writing is a spiritual breeze of beautiful, heartfelt and inspiring words that transcend the soul."
Isabel Puente, La Coruna, Spain

"Suhail is an amazing writer. He is ahead of his time. He is as good as any master. He offers great insights into people's psyche and uplifts people with his words."
Aileen Kelly, Artist, Ireland

"Suhail takes your soul on a journey of self-discovery, stimulating forgotten, ignored and undiscovered emotions. His words push the pause button on life, allowing you to understand a deeper sense of being."
Reza Kalamadeen, Kuala Lumpur, Malaysia

"I have had the pleasure of reading Suhail's insights and love his words; they give me much comfort. Suhail definitely encourages and inspires readers and followers to truly go within themselves to examine their consciousness. His writing makes a profound difference in my everyday life and strikes a chord deep within me. Suhail is very intuitive and his work is balm to my soul."
Veronica Forster, Melbourne, Australia

"Suhail has changed for the better since he began his spiritual exploration in greater depth over the past few years.

He is more thoughtful, more loving and always open to listen and learn. He is very kind, generous and loving. I am very lucky to know him and count him as a friend.
Caroline Kendal, England, UK

"Suhail is the alchemist of words. I'm often left spellbound by his transformative messages. Don't be surprised if you find yourself longing for his next insight. I can't get enough of his magical concoctions, each a healing elixir for the soul."
AJ Beaber, Author of You & I, Inc. Founder of Ignite The Light, Denver, Colorado, USA

"Suhail's writings are drawn from the teachings of all the world's great philosophies. However, what makes Suhail stand out for me from all the others is that his words come from a man whose own life experiences help to "bring home" his spiritual message and gives them so much more meaning. To study and absorb his thoughts provides the reader with both strength, optimism and determination to overcome the challenging issues that we all face in life."
Rowland Gee, London, England UK

"I love to read every single word of Suhail's writing. It is gorgeous. His words deeply impact my heart. His spiritually poetic writing transforms and is full of love and light."
Carmen Scherer, Lake Constance, Germany

Suhail's writing is full of wisdom which is infused with an abundance of empathy and is all tied together in a warm

spiritual cord which we all want to grab onto. His writing is endlessly uplifting and good for the soul in this ever-changing world."
Max Grafftey-Smith, Dubai, UAE

"Suhail's words have inspired and helped me through my difficult times. He is a truly spiritual person and it is like a magical experience to read his healing writing."
Julie Bruce, Perth, Australia

"Like poetry that soothes the soul, Suhail's powerful thoughts and messages remind us of the need to reflect on our personal journey toward inner peace and love. Thoughtful and powerful insights written with humbleness and love."
Maria Isabel Datiz Stevens, San Juan, Puerto Rico

"Suhail produces beautiful, heart centred writing. It comes from a very soft place in the heart which beats with butterfly wings of the Divine Feminine. Many other women feel the purity and romanticism of his words. They are like a balm to the heart. He writes about Divine Love and the Beloved and the energy is very much like Rumi and Mystical Sufism. He is a beautiful soul."
Tamara Bahar, Roswell, Georgia, USA

"In recent years I have seen a significant transformation in Suhail's spiritual journey. I can safely say that he is now walking humbly, meekly, trustfully before God. He has taught and shown me that the Creator should be our only true example in life. I am so happy to have him as a friend."
Leroy Churchill Thompson, London, England, UK.

"Suhail is an extraordinary spiritual writer much like Rumi. His writings come from the purity of his heart and make us aware of the importance of spiritual intimacy, the understanding of consciousness and our connectedness to all things. Suhail's work ignited my heart and soul and has impacted my life in a profound way. His work is important and should be heard by all."
Ashleigh Patrice Brenton, Loveland, Colorado, USA

"Suhail's words not only touch a deep part of the soul; they also make the heart flutter. Suhail's words help create a deep connection to one's true self. His writing is filled with grace and humility that touches all.."
Michelle Bugeja, Queensland. Australia

"Suhail's writing is a way to bring truths, enlightenment and understanding to people. His work is centred in the depths of the heart that plants the seeds of wisdom that leads to life. His writing leads many to the great Light of Love."
Linda Masalkhi, USA

A PERSONAL INVITATION TO THE READER

IF YOU HAVE EVER BEEN FACED WITH A CRISIS OF MEANING THIS BOOK IS FOR YOU

This book shares my personal journey from such a crisis of meaning and place of darkness to a place of light and Love. I set out details of this journey and list 10 steps that I took to reach the Light.

These same steps are ones which you too can take. The 10 steps move you from the "path of knowledge" to the "path of action" and then to the "path of love". The book shares how I was able to complete each of these steps and what I needed to do within each one. You are invited to take these same steps if you wish to find the foundation of Traditional Wisdom which is the key that can unlock the cage within which so many of us have fallen.

By following these 10 steps you will learn:

- How to move from a place of meaninglessness and your own"dark night of the soul" to one of joyous purposefulness through unveiling the Light within your heart
- That it is never too late to begin to make this transformation provided you are prepared to be self-authentic and courageous enough to shed the veils of deceit within and around you
- How leading with your Light you make Love and Truth te foundations of all your relationships and most importantly the one with your true self.

The book sets out each of the steps with clarity and shares suggestions about how you too can follow these steps in your own journey. The 10 steps are summarised throughout the book

(including in chapters 3 and 12) and also in Appendix Two at the end of the book.

"Many Mansions" unveils the timelessness of Traditional Wisdom; leading to a rediscovery of who we truly are, our place in Creation and how we are each uniquely brave as well as beautiful enough to deserve bountiful joy.

ABOUT THE AUTHOR

Suhail Mirza graduated in law from the London School of Economics and then began a career as an employment rights lawyer in the UK. He represented those facing discrimination and unfair treatment in the workplace.

Several years later Suhail took the decision to enter the world of business. Within the UK Staffing sector, he is a well-known and respected figure; he wrote the acclaimed "Meet the CEO" book in 2016, serves as City Editor for the leading trade journal "Recruitment International" and is Chairman of two recruitment businesses.

He was also a co-owner of a family business providing adult social care which employed over 250 people prior to its sale. He has written for respected trade journals in healthcare for over a decade.

A few years ago Suhail was faced with a crisis of meaning and despite all the trappings of worldly success his despair lead him to question the value of his existence. Only when he rediscovered the timeless principles of Traditional Wisdom could his personal transformation begin. This required him to face his deepest pain and thereafter take the 10 steps of the "spiritual solution" and walk along the paths of knowledge, action and love.

Suhail founded "Spiritual Solutions" in 2018 as a platform for anyone who, like him, is facing a crisis of meaning. The platform offers resources to undertake the same journey from darkness to light that Suhail has taken in recent years.

Suhail wrote "Many Mansions" to capture the 10 steps of the "Spiritual Solution" in response to numerous enquiries from friends and contacts around the world after they had heard about his journey.

He has created an audio programme (also entitled "Many Mansions") in which he personally takes people through each of the 10 steps of "The Spiritual Solution" and his journey.

FOREWORD

We are all searching for the Eternal truth that will set us free from the chains of this world and propel us into the hemispheres of our soul.

Acceptance of our real being is the key that unlocks the pathways to the ever blessed heavenly and celestial worlds. Where we are in total union with the sacred and Holy manifestation of the Creator; where the reason for our existence came into being from pre eternity towards the never ending rivers of paradise that water our very essence.

The question on everyone's lips during this and many other lifetimes remains the same: How do we reach this state of equilibrium and awakening of the Divine within us, that beckons our spirit within each breath.

In every moment we are asking

- from which river of paradise do we drink to quench the thirst that we have felt since we placed our footsteps on this earth?

- Which path do we travel upon to find the meaning of our life?

- In whose eyes do we see the promise of love?

My own journey as the ever eternal traveller upon the road of love, has led me to embrace the hand of many mystical and spiritual teachers, sages and ascetics. Each have shone their glorious light upon my life and led me upon the path of the sacred journey of the soul.

Once you have been in the company of such gracious and highly evolved spiritual beings, one's thirst of the ethereal grows even stronger and the search intensifies.
What also becomes apparent in the physical world is that without these meetings with remarkable spirits life can become meaningless.

One such unexpected meeting with an elevated being was undoubtedly my meeting with Suhail Mirza.

I fully believe without any doubt that all such encounters are perfectly planned on the preserved tablet of fate. They happen when we least expect them, yet at exactly the right time that we were promised in the spiritual realms. Accordingly, such meetings have the greatest impact on our lives.

I have indeed been graced and honoured to meet the splendid soul and devoted heart of Suhail.

When he presented his book "Many Mansions" to me, I instinctively felt that within my hands I was holding beautiful and awe-inspiring heavenly inspirations.

I also knew that this book was going to be transformational for anyone that read it. The words contained within "Many Mansions" take you from the darkness of the night to the daybreak of hope.

It is as if Suhail hears the laments of our sorrowful heart and sings with the voice of the nightingale with his poetic, mystical and tender notes playing the music that we long to hear, that remind us of ourselves once more.

Suhail has a subtle yet powerful way of taking your hand and guiding you upon the three paths (of Knowledge, Action and Love) while gently encouraging you to implement the 10 steps of the Spiritual Solution that inspire and awaken you to take the road to self-realisation.

Within each of the 10 Steps that you embark upon there is another part of yourself to explore, to make peace with, and another cavern of treasure waiting to be found.

One must be brave to pursue this way of the heart, but in doing so, one becomes victorious beyond measure.

Suhail's presence and guidance throughout the illuminating pages of "Many Mansions" is a bridge between the realms of the spiritual worlds and that of the physical realms. The book brings all, who read the jewels of his wisdom, closer to the answer they have spent a lifetime searching; that we are all the quintessence of love.

Mimi Novic, Inspirational Author, Writer, Life Coach, Complementary Medical Practitioner, Motivational Speaker.
London UK

CONTENTS

Introduction	1
PART A: My Fall into Darkness	
Chapter 1: Paradox of the Present	12
Chapter 2: My Story: The First Dark Night	22
Chapter 3: The Spiritual Solution- 3 paths and 10 steps	44
PART B: Learning to see with our heart	
The Path of Knowledge	
Chapter 4: The Betrayal of Wisdom	54
Chapter 5: Reclaiming Traditional Wisdom	65
Chapter 6: The Treasure of Healing	81
- The Spiritual Solution – steps 1 and 3	
The Path of Action	
Chapter 7: Polishing our Heart	98
- The Spiritual Solution – steps 4 and 5	
Chapter 8: Forgiveness	114
- The spiritual solution- step 6	
The Path of Love	
Chapter 9: Awakening Authenticity	123
- The Spiritual Solution – steps 7 and 8	
Chapter 10: Letting Light Lead	147
- The Spiritual Solution – steps 9 and 10	

PART C: Living in Wisdom
Chapter 11: Trials of Transformation   163

Chapter 12: Faith in our Future   173
APPENDIX 1: Suggested Reading   185

APPENDIX 2: The Spiritual Solution Summary   188

Introduction

Being bereft of hope and enveloped in a darkness and despair that promises its unceasing company is a path few of us would chose to undertake. Seldom is the choice entirely ours however and life often gives us little warning of the lessons it wishes us to learn.

Though it now seems a lifetime away, only a few short years ago, Providence conspired to wrench me from my slumber and invite me to make a journey I had long known I must make. That was a journey to the centre of my being; to those places which we know exist but which we seldom acknowledge in the daily freneticism of modern day life. The journey would indeed lead me to the depths of despair.

There were so many times along that path when the voice within, felt compelled, to ask me whether my existence had any value; whether my life had any purpose or meaning. Was there any difference at all between being here or not. It was a place of falling. Of a loss of boundaries. The very predicates upon which to even ask questions about my existence had melted away.

It was as if the cardinal points on a map, to orientate oneself, to find a direction and traverse the terrain of life, had been erased. Leaving a void. Blank and boundless space. The inner turmoil lead to a place seemingly barren and unforgiving.

"There were so many times along that path when the voice within, felt compelled, to ask me whether my existence had any value; whether my life had any purpose or meaning."

Outwardly my life had all the trappings of success as defined by our ever more vacuous and ephemeral culture. Well known and respected in the business sector, physically healthy, blessed with many friends and a loving wider family. Yet long have we been cautioned not to judge a book by its cover; for only the drama being played out within bears true testimony to the truth of what the book contains.

Everything and Nothing

Those that choose to remain blind to the collapse in values (and that which is eternal) in our culture must need to continue in their quest for unceasing acquisition and escape. For the vacuum so created must be filled lest we confront the emptiness that would face us.

Our narratives tell us we are ever more masters of the universe in which we exist, that we have never enjoyed so much with which to satiate our pleasures. The tool of ever more complex technology, ours, to subjugate the flora and fauna of the earth; and also to keep us ceaselessly entertained and even turn back the hands of time and find the elixir of the vigour of youth. We "know" so much. So many "facts". Information is unceasing. The "data" can even be subject to sophisticated logarithmic programmes; such that those that hold its keys may now, in each moment, direct the masses to that which will make us "happy".

Yet we who see with eyes wide open notice the atomisation of life; neighbours with whom we have no contact. Faceless people who pass others by without any change in their countenance. The academics write of "ennui" or "alienation". But to ever more of us our world is shattering into fragments and innumerable and conflicting "philosophies" so the very concept of being a "person" is lost. Invited on the one hand to deify ourselves our mantra of modernism has plunged us into an abyss where nothing is certain. All values a negotiation subject to the whims of the moment. The spirt of an age that exiles Spirit itself.

Those that are awakening to the deadening effect of this loss of value will seek to fill the vacuum created by the extinguishing of that which is eternal. Many are the promises made by contemporary teachers offering lightening like paths to meaning and "success".

The path we ultimately choose carries heavy consequences.

At stake is the transformation from a place where "no-thing" has any eternal value or meaning; to a place where "every- thing" is a sign or symbol of a Higher Guidance. This wisdom is open to us to access if we are prepared to make the journey within and above.

"Invited…to deify ourselves, our mantra of modernism has plunged us into an abyss where nothing is certain. The spirt of an age that exiles Spirit itself."

Finding Me and Meaning

When I found myself in my own "dark night(s) of the soul" and felt lost and close to hopelessness I fell to my knees and asked for such (or indeed any) guidance. Despite long years drowned in the nihilism of an "advanced" economy still seeking to come to terms with its loss of empire and world influence I was blessed to recall that there existed a promise; within the various Traditions of Wisdom. A promise of a true philosophy able to provide meaning and return us to our true nature.

Initially my search, though earnest and even desperate in its desire to escape the darkness and abyss into which I had fallen, lead to so many frustrations. For the best of Modernism's knowledge claims lead me to innumerable dead ends.

By what can only be described as an act of merciful guidance (and a series of "coincidences" which of course I now know to be part of the perfect purpose of Providence) I was eventually lead to the door opening upon the inner truth common to all Traditional Wisdom. My transformation toward unlocking the Light of the Worlds within my heart had begun.

Over the course of several years I undertook three paths that have led to the polishing of my heart and complete transformation. A transformation such that if a spiritual MRI scan were possible it would show a spirit that today is totally alien to the person I had allowed myself to become at the start of this journey.

So completely changed I can now see with the pristine vision of the heart. It reveals the chains of fear, inauthenticity and crucially the very temptations offered by the "paths of least resistance" (which had formerly kept me a slave in destructive bondage) for the toxins they were to my spirit. All but extinguished these formerly intimate companions are lessons I wish had never had to learn. Yet as monuments they serve as a reminder that even the most overpowering of false edifices can be reduced to rubble by the power of love and truth.

My transformation has required walking the:

- The path of knowledge which leads to the awe of true awakening
- The path of action which leads to the power of inner prayer
- The path of Love which leads to the strength of surrender

These paths have lead me to meet some of the leading scholars of spirituality in the world who have kindly met with me and shared their insights and in some cases the Light in their heart. Some have become friends and true teachers. Scarcely deserving of such divine gifts as one previously so lost, I am and shall endeavour to remain forever humbled by such largesse from Heaven.

The journey in reality has lead me from one beginning to an ending leading to another beginning. The journey I have made and described in the book is *simple;* yet I must strike a note of caution that "simple" should *not* in any manner be thought of as a synonym for *easy.* For the years of striving have not been easy. Anything but. When you reach the depths of darkness within the human soul there is a seemingly infinite mountain to climb, in order to escape the shadows enveloping your heart. Many were the hours and days when the voice of doubt mocked my efforts to escape the prison which I had made my abode.

Yet I faced the darkness, denigration and doubt of the voice within; eventually it was drowned out by the music of Divine mercy and I emerged into the Light which guides me still. Would that it should do so for all the time I have remaining. So many more stations in my journey there are still to reach.

"When you reach the depths of darkness within the human soul there is a seemingly infinite mountain to climb to escape the shadows enveloping your heart."

That you will be tested along the way is an incontrovertible truism; the rewards are so great who can doubt a price will be demanded? Little did I realise at the time I began how severely I would be tested. That came several years after my wandering had begun and became a defining moment of truth within the journey of transformation.

Yet what I sincerely can promise from my heart to yours is that such transformation is on offer each day. For on that day when you are prepared to strive toward it, the forces ordering all the realms of existence shall respond in kind. As you ascend, so heaven shall descend; to lift you to the angel-ship that has always resided within you.

The path to transformation is open to you

For this is not the path preserved for the privileged few or requiring august institutions' dispensation in order for you to find your truth. You are the agent of your spiritual truth; for this is part of The Truth that resides within your heart. Awaiting reclamation. Indeed, it cannot know rest until such union is sought with the ardour of all your heart.

By following the 10 steps set out in this book, which take you to the path of knowledge, action and love, you too can be transformed and perhaps experience some of the most important benefits that I have been blessed to receive:

- Ever more at peace within, notwithstanding the severest tests of life
- Greater joy and happiness in the everyday events of life
- Gratitude becoming an effortless flow in all aspects of my being
- The courage to be vulnerable in all relationships
- Being able to Lead with love in all areas of my life
- Never feeling alone or loneliness within the depths of my heart
- Virtue, honour and truth becoming the foundation of all my actions

- Slaying the destructive habits and behaviours that had once been so dominant
- Being able to be true to myself and always speaking my truth, no matter what
- Knowing that there is but one Light and that it lies within my heart always

"You are the agent of your spiritual truth; for this is part of The Truth that resides within your heart. Awaiting reclamation."

Let us journey together

Below I set out the "roadmap" for the contents of the book. I trust this will help you perhaps by way of a checklist of the 10 steps that you will need to undertake if you wish to move from darkness to light. The first 3 steps fall within the "path of knowledge", the next 3 steps within the "path of action" and the final 4 steps within the "path of love."

The book is divided into three segments.

Part A ("My Fall into Darkness"): *Chapters 1,2 and 3*

- begins with chapter 1 setting out the way in which the ceaseless allurement of modernism has led to a shattering (of that which is eternal) both within our hearts and in our world.
- In chapter 2 I share in detail how I found myself drowned in such a world and the forces that contributed

to the loss of meaning which lead me to a place of emptiness.
- Chapter 3 summarises the way I was guided out of the darkness based on the three paths and 10 steps.

Part B (**"Learning to see with our Heart"**) sets out the 10 steps contained within the three paths of knowledge, action and love which helped me reach the Light within.

- *The Path of Knowledge: chapters 4,5 and 6.*
- You will gain an insight into the areas of study that prepared the foundation for releasing the transforming energy of Traditional Wisdom within my heart (chapters 4 and 5).
- The way in which the tenets of Traditional Wisdom freed my spirit by inviting me to look up, around and within is the subject of chapter 6. This "orientation" and "mode of being" is essential for the transformation and removal of the darkness from our heart.
- *The path of Action: chapters 7 and 8*
- knowledge alone (though vital to ensuring our foundation is strong) cannot be the basis to reach the Infinite Light. Chapters 7 and 8 outline the often painful but profoundly empowering process of polishing our heart. This includes looking in the mirror of our lives and how, through sincere contrition and forgiveness (chapter 8), we can purify our heart sufficiently to permit the Light within to once more illumine our path.
- *The Path of Love: chapters 9 and 10*
- the first two paths bring you to edge of time. True transformation can only reveal itself if you can take a leap into the sweetness of eternity; and do so with fulsome Faith even amidst facing (in my case)

emotional shattering so unexpected and engulfing. Chapter 9 outlines the importance of leading with love and being true to oneself as a means to healing. Chapter 10 completes the ten steps by revealing how honouring abundance and serving others ensures we fulsomely embark on the path of love.

Part C ("Living in Wisdom"): *chapters 11 and 12*

- brings perspective to our journey by firstly (in chapter 11) offering guidance in respect of the inevitable pitfalls and challenges we will face once we have truly begun our inner journey.
- Chapter 12 concludes the book with an outline of the next steps we can all take within the paths of knowledge, action and love today. And this chapter also contains a call for all who lead with love to fight the spiritual battle, within and around us, against the forces of the totalitarian claims of politics, scientism and religion when they each become fundamentalisms.

I am so honoured to be able to share the content of the journey I have undertaken and I pray that what follows helps anyone who may be struggling in darkness to find their beautiful light within.

So I offer prayers of Love and Light on your journey and it is my hope we are one day able to meet in person and share our stories with one another. Until then please know that we are one and united and through our dreams and prayers can unite in love at all times.

PART A: MY FALL INTO DARKNESS

CHAPTER 1
Paradox of the Present

Summary: In our world of plenty there is so much for which to be grateful. Economic, political and technological advances that our forebears could hardly have dared to dream. Yet amidst the "progress" more and more people are asking what price has been exacted by our domination of the created realm. For the ephemeral seems to have triumphed over that which is eternal. Yet if we search for the light within, thereby following the deepest yearnings of our heart, we can find a path out of the shadows.

So much we were promised in our salad days; that these times of modernity were the conveyance of such privilege for which we must offer supplication each day. That we the moderns have so much more than our forebears whose struggle with the everyday of life was marred by solitariness, brutality, brevity and desperate struggle. Such a contrast to the shimmering glory of our world today.

Certainly we are the benefactors of the genius which preceded us; that lead to the minds and souls who looked up to the starry heaven and found order and laws that offered insight into the Divine Mind. Gratitude is indeed due to these giants whose shoulders bear so much for which we take granted; health and wealth bestowed on the masses, whose aspirations have been filled with dreams of success, now accessible to so many more when compared even to the days of our recent history.

Through struggle we can also celebrate the greater inclusiveness for so many groups, in parts of our world at least. In the ability to participate in the very citadels of power which were formerly the preserve of those born to privilege and sometimes paternalistic pride. Fought with blood and the very breath of life we can shed our tears in memory of the martyrs for this cause; who were assured only of reactionary resistance and certainly without prospect of an easy triumph.

"Certainly we are the benefactors of the genius which preceded us; Gratitude is indeed due to these giants whose shoulders bear so much for which we take granted"

Let us not overlook economic and industrial production unimaginable at the commencement of the modern period which has continued to our day. Lauded indeed is the lifting up of so many from the ravages of poverty in recent decades. So many of us in the "advanced" economies now take the amenities of life and its comforts for granted; so much so that our future generations now see access to these as an inalienable right. Without in some cases giving the equal weight required to the responsibilities which must surely accompany all rights claimed.

Yet even at this moment of seeming triumph in the economic realm we must remain vigilant. For even as we celebrate the wondrous fruit of the philosophy of economic interdependence (as the key to prosperity) we today witness a reversion to more combative times. Where trade is wielded as a weapon and might is equated, once again, with right. Ours is the call to highlight the folly of such rhetoric.

The Price of "Progress"

Memory persists. As ever more shimmering stratospheric structures collude to overwhelm our vision of the skies. It seems that the human need for reconstruction of the Tower of Babel has never ceased though the language of its construction surely has. The memory that our modern period has also seen a descent. Into barbarity that even the most oppressive from written history would have struggled to imagine.

The Age of Empire betrayed the darkness in the human heart. Renting asunder the mythic promotion of the Idea of Progress. Some of the branches of Science (which had given us the power over the created Order which Prometheus could only have dreamt of possessing) turned humanity, with the aid of perverse philosophies, into a Deity. In whose gift was deemed the determination of the very value of their fellow humans; some of whom were determined to be less evolved. And whose existence was deemed no longer to represent the beauty of Heaven. But rather a retarded development rendering them not servants of but One Lord but servants to those who wielded the instruments of destruction (military, political and ideological) most ruthlessly.

The promise of technology and the Information Age now offers parallel universes of virtual brilliance and a panoply of possibility; even as so many in the maelstrom of modernity fail to take time to notice the unequalled beauty of Nature itself. A Nature whose ravaging we continue unabated simply to fill the void in our frenetic activity-dominated existence.

So wedded to our conspicuous consumption and mastery of the created realm we whose hearts "see" beyond the surface witness mass suffering. Such suffering which often manifests in the outer collapse of all that was once held sacred.

"The Age of Empire betrayed the darkness in the human heart and rent asunder the mythic promotion of the Idea of Progress."

Levels of depression, loneliness and addiction now dominate our media headlines as any notions of natural law and timeless truths lay buried under the juggernaut of modernism; that machine of modernism seeking to empty the content of values and vows once held to be covenantal with Heaven itself.

Even the innocence of childhood recedes into ever more compressed time. Subject now to the overwhelm and searing judgment of instant connectedness. The privacy of the home breached under the welter of a digital world; all just one click away.

Debauched imagery and debased iconography sullies even the most intimate episodes of human life. Those times when we should be able to transcend the demands of the moment and glimpse the eternal are now displayed on media for all ages to see. Intimate relationships are so often rendered commodified artefacts to amuse us via our digital devices. Where mechanics replace meaning, shallow surface outweighs depth and the quantity of transient ties are honoured over the quality of the eternal union of two hearts forged in timeless values.

The bounty of productive prowess has itself been exalted into the measure of human flourishing; poverty devoid of all honour. Lauded is a hierarchy occupied by ever fewer whose demands for ever greater dominance has in many places transformed the language of democracy into a vulgar plutocracy without even the semblance of shame.

Growing numbers however now feel a sense of loss at this inversion of our world. A loss of something fundamental; that which we deep in our hearts know must needs be restored in order to prevent the deeper inversion of the world we see around us. A world turned inside out where the exquisite balance and order of creation is replaced by a will to power under the seductive deceit that we are all now that "Super Man" who can control all.

Answering the call of the Heart

The sense of loss persists and is fuelled by the collective memory within our hearts of what is truly valuable to our sense of self.

Nature abhors a vacuum and the gap that is at the centre of each and all of us must find a medium that will occupy it; a proliferation of answers is offered by many self-styled experts often with promises of rapid transformation and success. These manuals fill our bookstore shelves, popular television and digital platforms ever more ubiquitously.
On offer are paths to greater happiness and fulfilment;

incredible relationships and transformed ever youthful physical bodies; unending financial success and career significance and even instant fame and favour.

"Growing numbers however now feel a sense of loss within this inversion. A loss of something fundamental."

And in our Age where instant gratification is deemed a right and outcomes must be delivered to our door (without our being inconvenienced from our relentless pursuit of happiness) so many "solutions" suggest that we can "fix" challenges at lightning speed. Mantras, retreats and high octane energy filled instruction mean we are a few simple steps away from transformation; the search for the philosopher's stone (or for an other-worldly alchemist) replaced by the alpha and omega offered by the sages selling success.

Finding the Eternal amongst the ephemeral

Well intentioned no doubt are so many of these paths to the nirvana of fulfilment and happiness. Yet so many are rooted in the very predicates of a modern philosophy whose patrimony sees humanity itself as a mere accident of blind forces with no purpose or direction. Other than a direction and tendency toward ever greater disorder and chaos.

At best our modern philosophy views our beating hearts, discerning minds and yearning for connection and beauty as mere "epiphenomena"; unexpected by products of the mechanical movement of physical entities and systems without which we cease to have any meaning or indeed existence at all.

So however well-intentioned and beautifully marketed many of the paths to plenty may be; ultimately they become routes to the cul-de-sac of meaninglessness, purposelessness and directionless redolent of the philosophical assumptions that have come to dominate much of our world in recent decades.

While we can find tools to tame the "externals" of our life, including our bodies and minds, this is akin to only seeking to beautify and perfect the structure of existence; the house or abode of our existence if you will.

Traditional Wisdom Rediscovered

Yet there is so much more at stake. Indeed, everything. For our hearts are seeking solidity for the very foundation upon which the abode of our presence rests. If we can know that foundation and ensure its nature is recognised and nurtured, we may have a path to a more permanent fulfilment and joy; to Love itself.

Traditional Wisdom which has sustained humanity for millennia attests to the Spiritual Essence within us (as evidenced by the Light in our heart) as being the true timeless centre of our existence. Present in pre-eternity and destined to shine long after the present cycle of Time and Space have ceased, our Light or Spiritual Essence and its cultivation offers, according to Traditional Wisdom, a place of ever present peace and freedom.
It was to this timeless source that I finally turned when all

hope seemed lost; deep within there is a recollection within each of us that permits access to an abode where truths are not accommodations or subject to the whims of the current majority opinion. That abode resides in our hearts. It seeks our communion.

That wisdom has been captured over the ages by the great sages who have walked the path less travelled; sometimes at the cost of their own lives and even more often at the cost of being punished or ostracised.

"Traditional Wisdom which has sustained humanity for millennia attests to the Spiritual Essence within us…as being the true timeless centre of our existence."

For Traditional Wisdom posits that all the great Traditions of the world are akin to points on the circumference of a circle; outwardly distinct and even appearing contradictory with one another in terms of ritual, dogma and sacred texts. The "exoteric" of any Tradition must needs be variegated as it reflects the wondrous diversity and manifold distinctions of each peoples to whom it has been conveyed.

Yet this circle remains but one. And it is the radii leading from each point on its circumference which represent the inner or "esoteric" path within each Tradition; this is the path of the great seers, saints and mystics which represents a journey within their very heart. It is but the same journey for each –no matter the exterior cloak which each may wear- and the destination is but the same. The same centre point of that one circle.; the Source from which all and each of us and all other entities in the created realm come into being and to which we all, inevitably, shall return when our path here has ceased.

Following the Light when all is dark

At the point of my greatest despair several years ago (when every path of current knowledge seemed to lead me to dig an ever deeper well from which there seemed little salvation) it was this Traditional Wisdom that opened its doors.

Over the years (followings its guidance) its truths have lead me; to meet with some of the greatest teachers in the world of spirituality; to the texts from Christianity, Judaism and Islam long forgotten or little known generally today and; lead me upon a journey to my spiritual essence. Where at last I found the Love and answers that seemed so elusive on my "external" travels.

This is the path that lead to the cleansing of my heart, the polishing of the mirror containing the Light within. It led to a total transformation of my very character and finally to a place of peace and Love scarcely imaginable a few short years earlier.

I cannot promise that the path was easy or straightforward. When you have spent so long without the guidance of Traditional Wisdom it is a truly demanding path out of the wilderness of meaninglessness to one of illuminated purposefulness.

"This is the path that lead…. to a total transformation of my character and finally to a place of peace and love scarcely imaginable a few short years earlier."

What I can promise is that it is possible for even the most lost and forlorn (and perhaps self-designated unworthy) among us to find a way to answer our heart's deepest yearning. And ultimately to find answers to our deepest questions about who we truly are, what our mission is, how we can reclaim the awesome majesty for which we were created and; finally realise our potential for love in a world that may have made us cynical and untrusting.

In our next chapter I share in more detail my story of how that path of Traditional Wisdom has impacted my search for Light when I found myself in a place of almost complete darkness.

CHAPTER 2
MY STORY: THE FIRST DARK NIGHT

Summary: Despite many of the external trappings of "success" when a powerful blow was struck to my comfortable existence I discovered that the lifetime of study I had undertaken crumbled in the face of the emotional darkness into which I was violently plunged. For that study was almost all within the confines of modern knowledge and far from the bosom of Traditional Wisdom. Only when I reclaimed the light of that Wisdom (path of knowledge) could I muster the courage to purify my heart (path of action) sufficiently to embark truly on the journey home (path of love) to the light within.

During the course of my journey from a place of hopeless despair to one guided by the certainty of joy (that only Light from within can bring) perspective has afforded me a new vision of how that journey unfolded. I can now see *three* distinct occasions that Providence intervened to show me the way along the path of transformation. These three episodes were ruptures that brought pain and at times deep despair. Yet they acted to keep me on course toward that vista which the memory of my heart had retained.

According to Traditional Wisdom sometimes we remain blind to the lessons or signs that predominate everywhere around and within us; for the maelstrom of moment by moment living can indeed be overwhelming to our souls. Such is the frenetic pace of modern life that we struggle to breathe at times.

"My crisis of meaning was the product of two forces or currents that combined in that moment to destroy the vacuous certainties that I had taken for granted all my adult life."

The summer of 2012 was the departure point for my journey; what I now see as the first "dark night of the soul". It was an episode for which I was wholly unprepared. The events of that time left me questioning the very value of my existence and whether I or indeed anything had any meaning at all. This despite the fact that I had always "believed" that there was a Higher Power and Presence that ordered the world and its unfolding.

When the paradigms with which we see the world are brought into question however it is a place of pain; and such dislocation can often lead to self-destructive patterns of behaviour as we struggle to find significance and connection. In vain we seek to discern intelligible patterns within which to frame the events of our lives.

My crisis of meaning was the product of two forces or currents that combined in that moment to destroy the vacuous certainties that I had taken for granted all my adult life. One was internal and the other was an external force.

Let me begin with the internal cause of the loss of meaning and purpose. This lead to a feeling of falling and loss which even now makes me physically shudder given its intensity. I suspect that many years will pass before it can be encountered without any residual "re-living" of it.

Foundation built on sand

I have been a lifelong student and recognise that my heart has always yearned to know the deeper truths of life's existence. So after graduating from university and beginning a career as a lawyer I spent every spare moment I could find seeking to satiate this lust for knowledge. It was my hope that this might help me understand the meaning of my existence and that of the world.

Through the years my studies took me into the great subjects of modern scholarship; English and World Literature, Philosophy, History, Sociology, Linguistics, Anthropology, the Natural Sciences, Law, Psychology and of course Religion. I read voraciously and was always known as the man who was so "well read" and even erudite. My lower ego was inflated by these compliments and I managed to convince myself that such understanding was all I needed to continue to succeed in life.

I now know that I had been busy creating a great repository of "knowledge" and very little "wisdom". For long years I was to remain oblivious to this distinction; would that we could know earlier what later unveiling was to render so obvious! But oblivious I remained. Wisdom remaining only a fleeting companion during my years of busy pursuits.

For the truth to which I now bear witness is that the behaviour and actions and endeavours of my life were dedicated almost without exception to the pursuit of the ephemeral and transitory. Save perhaps the ardent argumentation that I would reserve for those times when my belief in Heaven was questioned.

The moments. The moments. The artefacts. One after the other. The linear dispensation of time in my life was strewn with these motifs. Even as I ran and ran faster and faster; after each and every transient experience. Whenever the inevitable vicissitudes of life brought pain or challenge I took that "path of least resistance" whenever the fork in the road presented itself. I served and honoured the lower ego within in each and every such moment. Falling deeper into that well which only those whose hearts have been sufficiently purified can even discern. I was indeed blind to such truths. My heart was encrusted by all that was opaque and that Light which bears witness to our true nature firmly encased within that opacity.

Incrementally I had become set adrift on the bliss of ignorance. All the "knowledge" that I had acquired was a veil to what was truly real. A veil that prevented me from confronting the shadows that had enveloped the light within my heart.

Unsolvable Tragic blow

I know this to be true as my philosophy- the frame, assumptions and tools for understanding we all need to traverse the landscape of life- was one built of sand. For it disintegrated as my life propelled into the darkness of the summer of 2012.

The external shock that befell me was one I could never have foreseen; it also presented a challenge to me and those that I loved most that seemed completely without the possibility of resolution or repair. It was a tragedy born on the foundation of self-deceit which came like a "thief in the night" and left me paralysed. The details matter not (and for legal reasons cannot be fully revealed) other than a course of action planned over many years revealed itself to have been erected on a profound deceit. With consequences that could reverberate for years and exact a continued and all-encompassing price for my family.

I recall vividly the panic and paralysis. The paucity of my personal philosophy and all the knowledge I had gained was laid bare. The tragedy seemed to underline the nagging doubt that had always persisted beneath the surface of my consciousness; that despite all the reading and study I had undertaken over the decades I had not opened my heart to that which was truly Real.

So as I felt overwhelmed by the possibility of a broken future with destructive emotional consequences for me and those I loved most. All seemed lost. Nothing certain to cling to that could act as a pole to balance the disorientation I felt was engulfing me. I groped for insights and wisdom from all I had learned to help me see some certainty beyond the crashing uncertainty now surrounding me. Yet I found the search for some comprehension was leading me to the darkness I feared most; that of a world with no meaning or purpose. A nihilism which would be a cage without a key.

Dominated by the paradigm of modernism (which posits only a material universe) the subjects that I had studied now revealed their emptiness *given the mode of being* in which I had approached them. Now biology offered only blind forces destroying the weak. Anthropology was Man as a by-product of the forces of materiality and the human drama seen as nothing more than desperately eking out an existence. History was simply one damn fact after another, one war after another, one people dominating another.

> *"Yet I found the search for some comprehension was leading me to the darkness I feared most; that of a world with no meaning or purpose."*

A Threadbare Rope

The external shock combined with the internal weakness of my "knowledge" left me stranded at the bottom of a well where I could see only darkness; the innumerable times I had walked the "path of least resistance "in my life had also left me with only destructive ways in which to find some meaning or certainty when faced with a crisis.

They would be useless when that crisis was one that was *existential* in nature. What became apparent was that I had fallen into the malaise of modernism; of making all that was ephemeral (people, places, things, labels, moments, thoughts, ideas and plans and values deriving from the mind alone) the determinants of my self-identity and indeed my self-worth.

I fell into an abyss of darkness which threatened my very sense of meaning. I was crushed to the point of depression and self- worth of such poverty. So low in fact that I permitted myself to accept standards of myself and of others acting toward me which would have been shocking to the outside world.

For on the "outside" my life looked "successful". I was respected widely in my business life, had a circle of valued close friends and innumerable contacts within the leading organisations in my business life. Materially my life had the trappings that placed me in a place of privilege. It is an irony most acute that my social status from all this would have been enviable to the demographic from which I had come in my childhood.

Yet perhaps like so many the inner turmoil within bore no resemblance to the surface perceived by others. For even those closest to me were taken by surprise when I shared the depths of my anguish and darkness. That period in my life has forever etched in my heart a reminder to offer kindness and warmth to all whom we meet; unbeknownst to us they too may be fighting the deepest of inner battles even as their visible lives betray no evidence of such inner turmoil.

Despite being at the bottom of a seemingly endless well, the rope that my philosophy and "knowledge" should have afforded as a means of escape was all but rendered threadbare. For this well was one where the very meaning and purpose of existence was at stake.

Knowledge without wisdom can easily become the ugliest of vanities. When I looked into the mirror of my heart it was the ugliness of modernism that was staring back at me.

And yet the residual strands of this rope that did remain

were the ones which were to prove to be the remnants from which I was able to rebuild a return to my spiritual centre.

My Search

And so I literally fell to my knees and asked the Universe to show me a sign to find a way out of the pain. I cried out loud to whoever was listening to admit I was lost. That I was like a boat out at sea without any sight of land. I admitted my own knowledge offered no compass to guide me to my True North.

"Knowledge without wisdom can easily become the ugliest of vanities."

Innumerable were the times that I sat alone in the small hours calling out for a sign or guidance. With a wry smile I now recall those nights when I found solace in the catharsis of ceaseless tears. Sometimes listening to the artists whose words and music were able to open the flood-gates (that I had had to hold back as I went about the duties of each day in business and personal life) of my despair.

Yet in amongst all the confusion and disorientation I had still managed to hold onto a little shard of the Light in my heart. That light managed to shine on that part of my memory and intellectual search whence my ultimate salvation would lie.

For I was fortunate in that I had in my quest for knowledge

read a number of texts which spoke of the wisdom which stood at the heart of the great Traditions. A wisdom which had perennially been the light for Man in our quest to find a path to that which is eternal.

I had read (sometimes more than once) the *words* of these texts. But true reading is a form of meditation which calls upon not only our minds but our hearts. Yet up to that point in my life my heart had been engulfed so much in the transient temptations of this world, that I had never penetrated the *spirit* animating these texts.

Traditional Wisdom teaches us that there is always beauty and love and Divinity within our hearts; common to all such gardens of beauty if we fail to tend to the needs of that which is alive we shall incrementally permit the withering of beauty to become overwhelming.

The texts and wisdom and practices which I had *read rationally* about may, indeed, have sought to penetrate and brighten by inner light; indeed, that is the function of Traditional Wisdom which is never a dead letter but comprises symbols that are alive with the creative breath of Heaven. Yet the dense forest of weeds I had permitted to crowd my inner garden of truth acted as an impermeable barrier to being touched by the grace of Truth.

Alone with the Alone

When one has endlessly journeyed along a path, however destructive, its familiarity can become a comfort blanket though in reality it may act more like a straight-jacket to our soul. So I vividly recall the almost physical weight seeking to pull me back, as I even considered finding a road to Traditional Wisdom to see whether it indeed could offer a path out of the darkness.

"Traditional Wisdom teaches us that there is always beauty and love and Divinity within our hearts"

A crucial turning point came from a conversation with my mother-an unlettered woman whose soul exudes kindness, compassion and Faith, who had to break her heart (for she loves her son more than I can imagine any parent loving a child) in helping me to confront my truth. I vividly recall how she mustered the candour to deliver the blow to my heart: "You are a man of Faith only in Name". It was all I could do to hide my sense of shame and piercing pain; for the truth she conveyed shattered the comfortable self-deceits that had allowed me to veil this truth.

That night I stayed awake into the early morning and decided that I would strip away all I had known and create a new beginning. To build from a *tabala rasa* and begin a search for Truth wherever it would take me. That I would leave no stone unturned in my quest to return to the heritage offered by Traditional Wisdom and find its deepest truths. For my heart knew that my salvation and the key to the cage I had permitted myself to be placed within lay in that perennial truth. I knew this would bring me into severe conflict with the muzzle of modernism and I decided that if it indeed did so then so be it.

,aths

ɔwledge

n in earnest on the "path of knowledge". Some 500 books over the next few years made the breakthrough into the barrier which surrounded and veiled my heart. Thence did I begin to connect with the Light of Truth which we all carry within.

This was no easy or straightforward endeavour. For I began in two places where I thought some semblance of wisdom might be found most swiftly. First was the modern academic subject of and approach to "Religious Studies"; where else to find the truth? And secondly I sought the counsel and to receive the comfort of those that spend their days ministering to their flock; Religious "leaders" and preachers and practitioners.

It is a wonder I did not simply fall into the deepest depression!

The former, the academic world of religious studies, has for much of its history been a discipline which de facto assumes that the very core of Faith, a transcendent realm and a Creator or creative force from which all realms emanate, is not worthy of serious attention. Instead Faith is reduced to be a function of psychology, anthropology, sociology or economics where it is but the output of a rational weighing of what offers most utility! More recent acceptance of admitting the phenomena of religious *experience* (or purported experience) as worthy of academic study has opened at least a fissure in its approach to the Real. Yet (largely) orthodox approaches to religious "science" are still found encased within the seemingly unassailable tenets of a world view which asserts that truth can only be equated with that which can be measured by Man.

In terms of the second place of my initial travels, the daunting doors of "organised" Faith offered little to help the darkness in my heart. Perhaps I searched not hard enough; almost everywhere I turned I was enjoined to carry out the liturgical practices prescribed and was assured that belief would return. Doctrinal discussions did not speak to my heart to assuage my pain. Arid, desiccated faith, however sophisticatedly constructed, failed to slake the thirst of this broken soul.

Nowhere did I see the chord that must surely connect the exterior to the interior; which in all Traditions is honoured as the true path to finding our spiritual essence.

And yet something did change even amidst the various dead ends which both of the above seemed to be leading me.

For mine was a soul which had spent so much time orientated to that which contemporary culture offered as quick fixes for our need for significance, variety, certainty and intimacy; for such a soul, the exposure to even the most exoteric rendering of the great Faith Traditions was like receiving crumbs of the sweetest bread to one on the point of starvation. The very act of searching, with ardour in my heart, for the Eternal itself started the re-orientation of my very *mode of being*. This changed the basis for everything else; how can we see the rising of the sun when we are facing in the wrong direction. I had now managed to find myself turning east at least!

The "path of knowledge" lead me eventually to the great

mystics and saints of spirituality whose lives, writings and examples have animated Judaism, Christianity and Islam; the trinity of Abrahamic Faiths that have created the foundation for the "Western" world and indeed have impacted deeply the wider world.

Some of the very greatest minds and people who have ever blessed this Earthly realm spoke of ascents to heaven and interior paths leading to a union with the Eternal. Esoteric their wisdom may have at times seemed; but either all these towering intellects and beautiful souls (whose spiritual chivalry sometimes lead to their martyrdom) were suffering from a perennial neurosis or perhaps, just maybe, they were the ones who had escaped the shadows of the cave and seen the vistas offered by following the heart?

The path of knowledge radically altered my belief and conviction of the nature of reality, what it meant to exist and what it meant to be human.

Path of Action

It also gave me the foundation to undertake the "path of action"; specifically, as I was able to place myself into an existence far richer, more purposeful and beautiful than the dead, blind and merciless one modernism's best teaching offered, I realised that Oneness was the core principle of all. It was Traditional Wisdom's "Theory of Everything". And a theory which did not need to limit its understanding to only a select few able to understand the abstruse mathematical models and assumptions underpinning "scientism's" attempt to explain all existence.
This path meant having the courage to *witness* all the

shadows of my life; to stand naked in the mirror of truth and watch the movie of memory play its course. Nothing left out. All revealed. From there *contrition* for so much became a categorical imperative; the heart which houses our spirit of Light, must be polished for the luminosity within to shine in its glory. Without contrition we cannot hope to polish away the opacity into which it may have fallen.

It was from there that the compassion of candour flowed into the fruit of forgiveness. Without self-honesty and confession, no contrition can crystallise and without contrition we cannot seek let alone hope, to recognise the fragrance of that true forgiveness forged in Faith.

The effect of all of the above was the drenching of my soul with the healing insight, energy and love of Traditional wisdom. Through the tears (of pain and joy) this wisdom brought forth I was able to wash away the veils of confusion and error. See the chasms in my current "knowledge" and replace it with "wisdom". In order to be human fully, surely it must be the case, that *sapientia* must precede and inform all our *scientia*.

Path of love

Over the course of several years all of the above moved to begin the transformation of the base metal of my soul into that much more worthy of the spiritual heritage of which I and all humanity is the inheritor.

My reading of Traditional Wisdom led me to meet some of great scholars across the world of spirituality and many shared their own journeys; their grace acted to mend that which was broken within me. In some cases, friendships developed and my dialogue with them continues. A blessing for which no measure can be made.

I returned to the core activity that all Traditional Wisdom requires as crucial for inner peace, love and truth; the power of prayer and the remembrance of the Divine as central to my daily undertakings. It was poignant and painful that the prayers I was now guided toward were those that I had come to almost forget, given the passage of time, since I had uttered their sacred cadences.

The practice of making the sacred central to my sense of self also acted as a reminder of the temporality which is earthly life; that we shall all one day pass from this realm.

Accordingly, following the entreaties of my heart, I also began to visit cemeteries when the time permitted. This was motivated by acceptance and embracing of the fact that one day we must walk through the door of death. I found peace and heartfelt compassion in my visits. Reading the headstones took me to the world of those who were now in an abode to which I too must return. The ephemerality of bodily life was manifest in the heartfelt narratives of the inscriptions on the headstones from those the deceased had left behind.

Sharing the details of my journey of recent years, with close friends, on the paths of knowledge and action, brought much balm to my soul. This acted as a reinforcement of the transformative power of Traditional Wisdom. All were gracious enough to listen and were encouraging of my efforts to transform.
Receiving so much sincere interest from friends, family and

business associates was, however, something of a double edged sword. Certainly it acted as an added impetus to continue on the path more zealously; and yet also, almost imperceptibly, it was a passage for pride to (at times) dominate a soul still only at the embryonic stages of shedding the darkness into which it had chosen to fall.

"The "path of love" meant I had to begin the return to my true nature; the true nature of all…As the special creations of the Infinite."

All journeys of transformation come with danger; the danger of "failure" (though there never really is failure on such truly transformative journeys- only "signs" to interpret) and also the danger that we stumble and fall. Into the inevitable obstacles that must be placed in our path. Surely we cannot expect that former acolytes entranced by the ephemeral shall be easily permitted to "apostatise" and turn to the light without a fight?

Plunging into Love's Path

For me the great test came at the point where, as I have stated above, the paths of knowledge and action had conferred upon me the great blessing of re-orientating my inner sight upward and within.

Thence came a coalescing of circumstances that befell me which constituted a second and even more overwhelming "dark night of the soul". I shall talk more about this in chapter 9 but suffice to say that it very nearly destroyed my soul. I faced an emotional shattering that I thought would never be visited upon me. I came to find it affecting my health so much that medical intervention would I fear be needed; though I knew this would have been a chimerical solution at best. For the true impairment was to my soul and heart for which allopathic medicine would be no more than a synthetic and exposed placebo.

And so I faced this further "dark night of the soul" filled with dread that it would lead to an abyss where the life I knew would potentially forever be impoverished and those which I held dearest would be seared in suffering.

Yet Providence decreed that my soul could bear more than this and days after the commencement of the true "dark night" above another challenge came to test my spirit, as my wife suffered a stroke which I witnessed as it occurred. Showing no predictors of such an event it came as a bolt out of the blue which threatened the wider family in a way for which none of us were prepared.

This was a test of my character. Of my commitment to the change I had begun years ago. It was also a test of my fortitude. Of my faith which was truly fundamental.

Would I be able to overcome the allure (surely false yet formidable in the force of its long foundation in my life) of the "path of least resistance"? The shadows beckoned again as a place of refuge from the haze of the bewilderment I felt. Bewilderment that was combined with the searing pain and helplessness which respectively were the fruits of the two calamities referred to above.

However, unlike the "dark night of the soul" years before (which acted as the catalyst for the commencement of my spiritual journey) this time I had, through the paths of knowledge and action, a rope to pull me out of the well of darkness.

And, with hindsight, I can now see that all the shattering and shadows of this period were simply the conveyance through which I was to be placed onto the path of love; that path which transcends all our knowledge and mental commitments however great each may be. For it is only when we surrender to love that we have the chance to make our transformation truly enduring.

A place of Light

Thus this time as the vessels of my heart broke they unleashed the pent up Light and love that reside in the Spirit which is the true essence of each of us. We who are created in the form and image of the Divine have this access to a ceaseless ocean of radiance which we so often either forget exists or else have only a dim recollection of as the distractions of modern life, covers over our luminosity.

"I can now see that all the shattering and shadows of this period were simply the conveyance through which I was to be placed onto the path of love;"

And so, as we shall see in more detail in chapter 9, I was able to face the tumult of this testing time with a fulsome heart whose guidance revealed the final four steps needed to truly undertake my journey upon the path of love.

For the path of love requires surrender and vulnerability. It means drawing up the bridge to our citadel and allowing the world, in its glorious paradox of perpetual oscillation between angelic beauty and demonic ugliness, to embrace our most treasured space; our heart.

For me this meant that I faced the dark night of the soul over many months by leading with love while respecting all other emotions. And also, faced with the potentially permanent loss of the life I knew on so many levels, to have the courage(finally)to be true to myself and always speak my truth.

The final components of the path of love offered even greater challenge and test. Being able to combine a disposition of gratitude and joyful acceptance in the face of even the darkest of times required a true leap of faith in all that I had learned of Traditional wisdom.

And it is then that we discover whether we truly have the "spiritual poverty" needed; where we empty the significance we attach to ourselves. In the face of the Awe and Power of the Divine. For only when we release that which we covet most- the feeding of our lower soul-are we led to freedom. A freedom that finds expression in the desire to serve others and save their pain and suffering; even as we are fighting our own inner turmoil in the face of an overpowering sense of desolation.

In this service to others we walk the path of the saints. We manifest the Mercy of the One in our own imperfect way and perhaps even momentarily transcend the wrenching pain and cries of our own ego and realise that this is transitory. Linear time is subsumed within Cosmic Time and we become creators in our service to others.

Never before had I been able to pour the love in my heart in such abundance in my interaction with friends, family and business associates. And also with people who were then strangers and have since become treasured friends across the world.

Freedom to be me

All of the above lead me for the first time in decades to be proud of me; in all my self-manifesting imperfections and idiosyncrasies. I was able to love myself enough to reveal who I am in all my dealings with people. Love was the grounding of all actions and truth the criterion guiding all my plans and efforts.

I had never known such liberty even if it was to be some months before the dark night of the soul was finally extinguished. To permit, no doubt, a new cycle of day and light to replace it.

Part of this transfiguration included being guided to social media and Facebook in particular. A medium I had derided for many years as being vacuous and frivolous. How wrong we can be! And another lesson in ensuring that humility permeates all our professed certitudes.
Certainly it was Faith, Family and Friends that were incalculable blessings in this passage from darkness to light

and true immersion in the "path of love"; social media also played a priceless part in the full embrace of love's path.

Within it I found a platform to pour out the pain in my heart and combine it with all the messages and voices in my soul that I had suppressed for long years; which suppression had incrementally and inexorably drained the *elan vital* from my being. It allowed me to give expression to the poetry I found hidden within my grief.

"And it is then that we discover whether we truly have the "spiritual poverty" needed; where we empty the significance we attach to ourselves."

Through social media I met wonderful friends and kindred souls around the world who found value in my words, who shared their own wisdom and love and whose embrace and energy helped to save my soul. Should Providence permit me to meet them in person, as I feel it surely will, I apologise to them in advance for when we embrace my tears of joy, gratitude and love may prove embarrassing to them!

Signposts of Serenity

There have been so many benefits to my pursuit of the spiritual path including the most priceless of all; the serenity of knowing that I am never alone and always loved by the Light which created all we see and feel; for that light shines within me and has always done so and shall endure until the end of the present cycle of time.

I have been blessed enough to be honoured, through my thirst to learn about Traditional Wisdom, to be invited to consider undertaking a PhD by one of the leading and most well-known scholars of Divinity in the UK.

And more recently in 2017 one of the world's leading scholars of spirituality (based in Spain) has helped map out a route whereby I may be able to undertake doctoral research looking at the common paths to union with the Divine across Judaism, Christianity and Islam.

Scarcely believable is it sometimes what Mercy can do and how grace can honour even the person most lost and distanced from the Light; with that most glorious of gifts, another opportunity for redemption. The door of the Divine is always open. Never is it too late to take the time to transform and reclaim our destiny; for we are all and each one of us both beautiful and brave. Deserving always are we of Heaven's endless bounty.

CHAPTER 3
SPIRITUAL SOLUTION: THREE PATHS AND 10 STEPS

Summary: *There are no "quick fixes" for true transformation from a crisis of meaning and place of darkness to the power of Faith and a place of Light. This shall be a journey that demands much but offers infinitely greater riches than the price it shall ask of you. The "Spiritual Solution" comprises traversing the paths of knowledge (steps 1-3), action (steps 4-6) and ultimately love (steps 7-10). When we reclaim the heritage of Traditional Wisdom we have a key to escape the cage of modernism. Each of the paths and indeed each of the 10 steps are relationally dynamic; as we undertake one path or take one step it enriches our experience of the other paths and steps.*

Wary we must be of those that offer seemingly easy and rapid paths to inner transformation and to the unveiling of the Light within; the greatest treasures demand that we are prepared to undertake the journey of the hero and overcome the greatest obstacles. Willing to pay whatever price for the priceless prize of peace.

And I wish to reiterate the comments made in the introduction; this book is but a meditation and a heartfelt plea of gratitude that I wish to share with the world. As one saved from the well of darkness I shared my journey with many others who were gracious enough to ask whether I planned to teach what I had learned. Whether I was prepared to guide others who may be facing a crisis of meaning and their own dark nights of the soul?

Their kind words emboldened me to bring together in a systematic way the 10 key steps that had comprised the three distinct paths that I had been guided to undertake. In order to make the journey of inner transformation and to learn to "see" with my heart.

Accordingly, all those that are kind enough to read the words of this book must also keep in mind this sincere plea: that whilst the change that I have discovered has been truly liberating for me- inevitable given the sheer extent of my erroneous wanderings over so many years- it remains an incontrovertible truth that the principles set out below are a beginning. An invitation, if you will, to re-orientate your life so as to commence the search for that which is eternal; and thereby be a shield against the prospects of being overwhelmed by the ephemeral so exalted in our day.

So as we stand at the very early stages of the path of wisdom it is with humility and honour that I share the three paths and 10 steps in the chapters that follow with the above caveats firmly in mind.

The next section of the book will take you step by step through the "Spiritual Solution" that has performed a miraculous transformation in my life and in my heart. It is my sincere prayer that these steps speak to your heart; and by following them you too find a path that takes you to your inner truth which ultimately remains firmly part of The Truth.

"Wary we must be of those that offer seemingly easy and rapid paths to inner transformation; the greatest treasures demand that we are prepared to undertake the journey of the hero and overcome the greatest obstacles"

The "Spiritual Solution" is founded on a sincere desire to find a deeper meaning to what we take for reality and search for the true Reality that frames our created world. It will cause us to become uncomfortable with so much we take for granted in the dominant cultural narrative of modernism. That "philosophy" that relies only upon discursive knowledge.

Walking on this path also requires us to become uncomfortable with ourselves and our lives, with our very sense of who we have permitted ourselves to become. Only by having the courage to be truly iconoclastic can we see the real you, the real me, the real we and the real us.

So let us "signpost" or map the contours of the three paths and ten steps. By following these 10 steps, which will take you across each of the paths of knowledge, action and love, you can find the inner light that has always shone within your heart.

SPIRITUAL SOLUTION: 3 PATHS AND 10 STEPS

The first stage in the journey demanded that I clear my mind as much as possible of what I had accepted as truth and challenge the very foundations of the way we are all taught to see the world in today's culture. This is the path of knowledge which includes the first three steps:

Path of Knowledge

The result of this path is our being able to reclaim the tenets of Traditional Wisdom. Before that it requires us to question and place our current knowledge of the world (dominated for most of us by the frame of modernism) in that wider context. This allows us to ask questions which unveil that which is constant and which underpins the world of permanent change around us. That foundation which does not diminish its luminous nourishment even if the external world we live within brings us its worst.

When we gather up such insights we can begin to "see" differently and this forms the foundation for all the other steps and paths. Only once I was able to see the Truth within this path of Knowledge was I able to have the confidence to know that I had a centre which would act as the pillar for all my actions; it would be a place to which I could always return whenever the inevitable doubt and challenges of life presented themselves.

The Spiritual Solution: Steps 1,2 and 3

The three steps within the path of knowledge are:

1. Learning to "Look up"- **Step 1**
   - Placing ourselves into a richer universe and understanding of existence we can find a deeper purpose and direction that is a pole around which the created and physical universe can be better understood and placed.

2. Learning to "Look around"- **Step 2**
   - Nature to which we are inextricably linked for this cycle of Time offers innumerable "signs" for those with eyes to see; signs of the true reality of our being and indeed all Being. And it will reveal the modes of Knowledge that are available to us.

3. Learning to "Looking within"- **Step 3**
   - This will unveil the nature of our mission as individuals and as a collectivity; This step will also help us to see the war that we wage within our very selves and how focus on what is everlasting within can make sense of our heart's striving. From this sacred anthropology we also find timeless values that are designed to guide us to our true selves.

The path of knowledge leads to an awakening. A new recognition that the world around us is perhaps turned inside out. That our accepted frames of reference are limiting in a way that strangles our unique ability to reflect the Divine beauty.

Yet knowledge takes us only to the outer perimeters of the paths we must take if we are truly to answer the call of our restless heart. That unveiling requires we act to polish the mirror that encases our heart; a mirror which may no longer truly reflect our light due to the shadows and debris we may have permitted to accumulate over the years of wandering.

Path of Action: Steps 4, 5 and 6

And so we are guided to undertake the path of action which itself comprises three further steps:

4. Witness and Confession- **Step 4**
   - Only when with searing self-honesty we confront the state of the heart we possess can we commence the uncovering of its Light. No stone must be left unturned. No door unopened. No lie uncovered.

5. Courage of Contrition – **Step 5**
   - Faced with our nakedness in front of the mirror of our soul's memory we have the chance to extinguish pride and self-deceits. When we rent asunder these veils we can confront the vulnerability of the revelations we have uncovered. And allow the tears to cleanse our pain and give expression to our sincerity and sorrow.

6. Faith in Forgiveness- **Step 6**
   - When we learn to forgive we revivify our lives. In that moment we can renew our covenant with the Infinite that orders all. This step outlines the importance of forgiving others but equally importantly forgiving ourselves. These are the key
     to unlocking the door to Love. "Signs" of surrender are manifested within us and around;

if we recognise them we free ourselves of pain, shame, hurt and fear.

There is no set time within which these steps will manifest as much will be determined by our sincerity and courage to face the dis-ease within our Spirit. Fortunate are the souls who are able to seamlessly move from the path of action to that of love and in their surrender unlock the Light in their hearts.

Mine was not such an exquisitely self-ordered journey. As I shared in the preceding chapter only when faced with an emotional shattering which asked the deepest questions about the extent of my commitment to self-truth was I guided to letting go and surrendering to the call of Love in my heart.

Path of Love – steps 7, 8, 9 and 10.

All Traditional Wisdom exalts the centrality of the path of love. For love is the highest theophany of the Sacred which we as humans can manifest. I discovered that the final 4 steps set out below were the indispensable handmaidens to any hope to enshrine forever the change that had begun to take place in the crucible of my healing heart.

7. Lead with Love & respecting all other emotions - **step 7**
    - When we are wounded, betrayed or in pain the path of Traditional Wisdom enjoins us to always nevertheless lead with love; remembering that, by also respecting all other emotions, we also let the world know however that our compassion is not to be confused with weakness

8. Always living our truth - **step 8**
    - If we have polished the mirror of our heart the Light within will reveal our self-truth; and demand that we always live by it in all areas of our life; no matter what the consequences.

9. Recognising boundless blessings – **step 9**
    - As our heart frees itself from the shadows of the past and the fears of the future we find a place in time that is eternal; and in that eternal moment, that unique present, we are able to give gratitude for the renewal we receive each day and throughout each unit of time

10. Serving others – **step 10**
    - Freed from the dominance of the lower soul/ego and recognising its false allures and shimmering promises we see Oneness in all of our lives and all worlds. We then move to pouring out the boundless love in our heart and serving others; so that it not only becomes a balm to our own pain but, in the most profound sense, we recognise such service as the highest form of self-love

"All Traditional Wisdom exalts the centrality of the path of love. For love is the highest theophany of the Sacred which we as humans can manifest."

The spiritual solution encapsulated by these 10 steps is open to each of us; whenever we are committed to transforming ourselves. The spirit that animates each of the ten steps within the solution comes from within us and not without. Embarking on the 10 steps without a sense of "spiritual chivalry" will doom us to be slain by the forces that keep us enslaved to our current paradigms; the very same (that in my case at least) lead to my crisis of meaning and the darkness that threatened to overwhelm me completely.

It is vital to remember of course that each path and each step stands in a dynamic relationship to each other. Once I had begun the reclamation of Traditional Wisdom I could truly take the six steps in both the paths of knowledge and action. To see the world and myself anew. Thereby to commence that inner purifying of my heart which is critical to permitting the light of the four steps of the path of love to truly infuse my every breath. Thence the journey continues through continually applying the ten steps each day.

In Part C of the book we shall share with you the likely challenges and obstacles you may face even after you have completed the 10 steps and arrived at the place where the Light within begins to once again illumine your decisions, thoughts, prayers and direction.

Be aware that you will indeed be tested and that the pitfalls and temptations (large and small) are virtually inevitable. Recognising these assailants is the subject of chapter 11.

Let us now consider each of the three paths and individual steps in more detail

PART B: LEARNING TO SEE WITH OUR HEART

THE PATH OF KNOWLEDGE

CHAPTER 4: THE BETRAYAL OF WISDOM

Summary: Modernism is currently the dominant "mode of being" across ever more parts of the world. It reduces our world and (perhaps even more importantly) each of us to accidents of blind and pitiless forces moving in a direction no one knows and without any purpose. It denigrates and marginalises that which is Eternal and seeks instead to Deify Man. Yet modernism has over the past centuries been the catalyst for catastrophic calamities and destruction. Not only of the world out there but to the inner world of being human. Yet it stands as an aberration and treacherous "philosophy" in its suppression of the timeless wisdom of sacred knowledge that has guided humanity for millennia. When we finally see this betrayal we can commence to construct the vision of Traditional Wisdom.

What happens to a people who forget their origin? Traditional Wisdom speaks of the people that shall perish in the absence of a vision.

So we must begin by seeking to understand what it is that we "see" when we look around us and deep within us. This is where my return from the darkness began. Too often we search frenetically for a cure all or method that will soothe our pain in the moment or the short term. We run from one tree to the next without ever stepping back to survey the forest.

"…each of the ten steps that I took to move from darkness to light are grounded in the principles and insights of Traditional Wisdom."

What is it then that we "see"? That will depend on not only the instruments we utilise but also the nature of our sight itself. If we are to perish without a vision surely, we owe it to ourselves, to understand whether we have truly been seeing all that there is or discover we have seen only a part of the picture?

In chapter 2 I shared some of the bewilderment I experienced as I searched for a path to find something eternal or everlasting in a world of change and transformation. And I also referred to some of the cul-de-sacs that I found myself trapped within as I reached for the knowledge across so many academic subjects.

In what follows in this chapter I want to expand in more detail about the "path of knowledge" so you can (I trust) be saved from some of the painful mistakes that I made. Appendix 1 ,at the end of this book, lists some of the texts I found most important in my journey and in the next chapter I shall share some of the deepest insights I discovered within Traditional Wisdom.

This is the very foundation of all that follows; each of the ten steps that I took to move from darkness to light are grounded in the principles and insights of Traditional Wisdom. Only when I was certain in my heart about this grounding could I hope to make permanent and real the transformation that I was undertaking.

For what was at stake, in all candour, was everything. Either nothing was permanent and all was contingent; one damn fact after another in our lives and in our history. No meaning or purpose. Or there was indeed something within us and above and all around that was eternal; that was Infinite; that was the Source of all procession and return.

What is known?

When the crisis of meaning engulfed me in the summer of 2012 I reached inevitably for the knowledge that was offered by the best and most "advanced" disciplines of our modern world. Philosophy, psychology, the natural sciences, the social sciences, information technology and anthropology etc.

The confidence of the current age surely gave us the best hope to find strength in times of our greatest weakness I had thought; we look at the icons of the modern age and see opulence and grandeur on a scale scarcely imaginable even a generation ago. Daily we are informed of the insights that the latest thinking and research can offer us individually or as a collectivity.

The central question for our knowledge platforms of today, what we call modernism, seems to be "what can be known?"

We break the visible realm into infinitesimally smaller constituent elements with the promise that through this slicing and dicing, the whole as a whole shall be revealed to us. We stretch back into the very commencement of our physical cosmological cradle and seek to discern in those fractions of a moment the source of all the complexity of our existence.

"The project of Modernism has over the past centuries - often with naked zeal and rarely with any humility- placed only that which can be measured by man as the arbiter of all truth."

As our theories of the universe become open to only those with the grasp of the most abstruse mathematics we posit ever more dimensions of existence in an effort to better understand but one, our own. Modernism's theories suggest only cold blind forces that propel the motion of matter to create the energies that animate the visible realm.

When I turned to the precepts of modernism- the assumptions that underpin the current lens through which we are enjoined (even cajoled) to see the world- I found there only the cold calculus of the rational mind.

The project of Modernism has over the past centuries -often with naked zeal and rarely with any humility- placed only that which can be measured by man as the arbiter of all truth. Knowledge confined to only that which our mind can grasp. The Reason of Man has been elevated to the summit of all. Mind has extinguished Heart; Sensory sight blinded Spirit's Secrets. Facts triumph over Faith.

Whence Wisdom?

Lest we forget, the greatest masters of Greek wisdom had advised that philosophy must begin our search for truth with a sense of wonder. They added that access to a higher realm would guide us to the truth which has always resided within us; all striving for wisdom being the reclamation of that which we already know.

Yet modernism's philosophers have now long taught that we must destroy any notion of other realms; that even if we may be defined ultimately by our Mind we are rooted forever in the physical. For that mind must needs be the product of the physical matter and energy which are the building blocks of all entities including us. This is the nature of our "being"; the coincidences of forces and motion in transient moments of time.

Perhaps no longer there remain those that define truth only upon the premise that it must be able to be positively measured by the mind of man; for their successors have permitted credence to be given to the *experience* of being human. Though they too see any human freedom of choice as being confined by the larger forces of history or culture. Into these directionless, purposeless forces, we are plunged, modernism claims, and though we can choose our response to them, we are ultimately rooted within their merciless procession.

Furthermore, as modernism strives to answer the question

of "what is known?" What becomes of "me", "you", "us", "we", all of us?

For it can be said that the modernism mantra of measurement and experiment may have left us with no "me" at all; no "self", or many "selves", or an "I" that changes and drifts as the product of the memories it can recall. Or perhaps the "me" I think I am can be equated to little more than a series of logarithms whose outputs we call behaviour or sense perception or emotions?

What of "We"? You and me? Us? What do modernism's masters have to offer as a beacon to guide us (as a collectivity) through the maelstrom of multiplicity that we see in a world of ever faster change and ever more global transformation?

Rational utility maximisers driven by the bargains that satiates our individual needs and wants is the answer for some; each of us atomistic actors, each playing our self-serving role in the drama of human history. All this atomic activity shall, we are assured, inexorably lead us to a blissful balance that leads to a better tomorrow for the collectivity in which we find ourselves. Furthermore, we are seen as entities seeking adaptive advantage even in our acts of heroism, compassion and morality. Ultimately modernism tells us that we each (and indeed all collectively) remain specks in a storm whose origin we can never know and whose ultimate end we can never predict.

What of Faith itself? The great Traditions whose tenets have permeated every society and civilisation? What of that which seems the perennial yearning within Man to find a bridge to the realm of the Real. That Reality, which all societies, preceding the birth of the modern, believed informs this realm and whose language long we have sought to decipher?

Modernism mocks those who profess such yearnings; perhaps not with the ardour and derision of yore, for our "subjective" experience of the holy, is now at least deemed worthy of detached study, classification and reductive explanation. Yet still Faith is seen by modernism with the paternalistic perspective that such yearnings will one day be seen as part of humanity's adolescence.

For it remains the contention of modernism that when we all are "Enlightened" we will as a species have finally arrived at our maturity; and in such adulthood, with Reason as our guide, we will be able to see the belief in the Eternal in all its nakedness or childish credulity.

As I was engulfed in my crisis of meaning and faith I realised (whilst it had been brought on by the external pain of my first "dark night of the soul") it was also the outcome of the very "knowledge" I had been accumulating over the years. For such knowledge virtually in its entirety was grounded in the assumptions of modernism set out above. I found in the hour of my greatest need the best of modernism left me without an anchor upon which to find orientation as the sea swirled around me during my crisis.

What if we were to turn the tables on modernism's claim to represent the ever more continual pinnacle of our evolutionary ascent? And remembering the precept "by their fruits ye shall know them" determine how its boast to represent the maturity of man measures up?

Modernism's Malady

Here we find that the mirror of modernism conveys an image of such distortion that surely we must soon declare that *it* is the one whose nakedness and covetousness has been laid bare?

For in the period since the so called demise of the Deity was declared by the philosopher's mad man, what have been the fruits humanity has yielded as our Reason has become ever more deified?

The global conflicts resulting in tens of millions of deaths with technology's finest and most "advanced" weaponry has been accompanied by the praying in aid of the "latest" knowledge to posit a hierarchy of human "races". Whence subjugation and exploitation on a scale equalling (if not surpassing) anything seen in humanity's so called 'medieval' age became justified in the name of the "religion" of modernism. The whole scale extermination of entire peoples has remained a feature of our world, centuries after the Age of Reason made its entry onto the stage of humanity's history.

The accelerated destruction of the very ground upon which all our destiny rests has also been a fruit of the project of modernism; Mother Nature ravaged by the rapacity that must be the corollary of the narrative, alluded to above, which sees the human as a rational pleasure maximising atomic actor. That sees no ghosts in the machine; no living force within flora and fauna. All "resources" at our pleasure to satiate our insatiable lust for consumption.

"Progress" once exalted as the heritage of the industrial and enlightened man now seen surely as a tragic and vacuous claim buried under the horrors of our Age? For in our techniques, of communication, travel, production and consumption surely our tools are indeed far more sophisticated than our ancestors. But the price exacted for such progress cannot be seen as negligible? Upon what calculus of utility can we claim a return for these endeavours?

"I found in the hour of my greatest need the best of modernism left me without an anchor in which to find orientation as the sea swirled around me during my crisis."

Consequences of our culture

The malady of the modern age has not gone unnoticed even amongst those for whom only the physical realm exists. In its most recent phase some of our very best minds now question whether we can *know* anything at all with any certainty. All fields of knowledge even those of the natural sciences are now cast in a new light.

For such thinkers' assert that there can be no "objectivity"; that all knowledge is mediated by the actions and beliefs and interests and pressures which affect those who produce any knowledge claim.

We have perhaps for the first time nakedly arrived at what must be the darkness in the heart of the modernism project; that nothing is more *real* than anything else. All knowledge is simply human construction. Edifices built, sincerely and honourably no doubt in most cases, upon the foundation that sees Man as the measure of all.

This is the world of Nihilism. The catastrophe of nihilism. Where there are no higher values which can definitively be viewed as such. For in this world even our values are seen as human constructions subject to the whim and ways of time and preferences of the collective desires in any moment. All is illusion. Ephemeral. Transient.

If we are indeed, in our humanity, no more than the emergent properties of physical processes within our biology; if we are limited only by the time during which we can function as physical organisms? Then whence love, beauty, truth, compassion?

For in the world defined by Modernism, we must be under no illusion, those that we love the most are forever lost to us when they pass from this realm. Our remembrances merely psychological tools to help us confront the finality of death. Our prayers for those who have passed reduced, by modernism, to empty platitudes, for no one is listening to such heartfelt supplications. The music of our heart playing in a pitiless vacuum for there is nothing beyond our being.

Yet can we really dismiss, such yearnings for a realm beyond this one, as nonsense, as modernism must require us to do? Can we really believe that those who have sacrificed their lives in their quest to teach love and compassion were nothing more than physical apocalyptic figures limited to their period of time?

"We have perhaps for the first time nakedly arrived at what must be the darkness in the heart of the modernism project; that nothing is more real than anything else."

Wisdom as remembrance

In the months following my crisis of faith I fell perhaps even deeper into despair. The bleakness and blankness of modernism offered no succour to my soul. So once again I faced the allures of my destructive "paths of least resistance" which seemed to offer the only reprieve (even if temporarily) to my pain.

My study of the "science of religion" lead me to become even more bereft of finding the Eternal. As this "science" reduced religion to sociology to psychology to biology to chemistry to physics; just another dead block of facts.

It is said that the darkest hour is before dawn. And for me this proved apposite on my path of knowledge. For I was reminded, even as greater and deeper despair threatened to make my crisis of meaning permanent, of the texts that I had read many years before. I recalled the works of many great minds, from history and indeed contemporary times, who offered a completely different view of the world.

Of the realms of existence (cosmology), the nature of existence (ontology) and the nature of being human (anthropology).

Among the texts and thinkers, I recalled were some of the very greatest minds in all human history. Though faint, my recollection was that they all believed in many realms of existence, of an infinite intelligence ordering all of reality, of our "being" as constituted within Being itself; and ascribing to our humanity the most privileged of roles within creation.

Either (if the claims of modernism were to be believed) such thinkers were deluded or suffering from a severe neurosis which rendered them capable of only uttering nonsense; or perhaps, just perhaps, these luminaries were actually the bearers of a Traditional Wisdom whose view of the world offered a key out of the cage.

And so it was that I committed to immerse myself in the teachings of Traditional Wisdom and follow its truth wherever it took me.

THE PATH OF KNOWLEDGE

CHAPTER 5: Reclaiming Traditional Wisdom

Summary: When we enter the timelessness of Traditional Wisdom we are enriched permanently. We find a whole order of existence that emanates from The One and a cosmology not blind and pitiless but one pulsating with purpose and above all cradled in Divine Love. We discover that all being(ontology) and existence is but part of a connected whole whose Being is the life force animating all creatures great and small. Furthermore, we look within and see not mere biology but the brilliant beauty of Heaven's special creation. For we are bestowed with the heritage to manifest the wondrous attributes of the Divine in this Earth at this time. Unity of existence, Oneness, is the perennial message of all Traditional Wisdom within which is grounded all the luminous multiplicity of creation.

The Teachers Appear

It is said that only like can know like; that within the disposition of the heart lies our receptivity to the Real. This truth was to become manifest in due course. What I did know from the depth of darkness into which I had fallen was that I had to open my heart fully. This was an imperative in order to understand the intent and spirit of the sages whose wisdom and works I knew offered a very different view of existence than that offered by the mandarins of modernism.

Even in my despair I found myself being pulled toward the vestigial Light in my heart. This seemed to be an inner response to the yearning I felt to be free from the crisis I was personally facing. At this time too I felt great unease at the growing coldness and anger that was being loosed upon the world as we progressed into the second decade of the 21st century.

Our "leaders" and "thinkers" had it seemed gone back in time too; but not to the sources of wisdom upon which our world was built. But gone back rather to the era of conflicts and hatred of barely a century earlier.

"It is said that only like can know like; that within the disposition of the heart lies the receptivity of the Real. What I did know from the depth of darkness into which I had fallen was that I had to open my heart fully."

Now we were being told that whole groups (comprising millions) of people were to be derided and marginalised; sometimes to be kept out by physical walls of hate and at other times by the walls of a belief system that saw clash and threat from anyone who failed to fully pay homage to "our" view of the world. Ever shriller have become the messages demanding we show no mercy to anyone "not with us"; whatever that meant. Asked to divide and deny the equality of our fellow man on the basis of a false creed of civilisational clash we had, it seemed, entered into a period I thought we had long consigned to the worst episodes of modern man.

So I turned my heart, mind and soul to the sources of the great Traditions. The revelatory repositories of our heritage to which so many had turned in their hour of need; to which so many owed their existence. That which was the bedrock of some of the greatest saints, thinkers and philosophers the world had ever known.

I drenched my life with the works of Traditional Wisdom. I wrote to teachers whose works helped me to restore my faith; those whose works placed the tenets of modernism in the context of millennia of human thought and spirit. And I learned that this spirit of Traditional Wisdom continued to live even as it faced the assault of modernism.

Scholars around the world provided the foundation for my rational return to faith. Space (and in some cases discretion) prevents me from listing all to whom I am indebted. I shall however seek to speak of those whose impact has endured over the years.

I had the honour, for example, of meeting with the wonderful Keith Ward, formerly Professor of Divinity at Oxford. Whose works on the true relationship between science and Faith opened my eyes to how Faith itself was the ground upon which some of the greatest "natural philosophers" had conducted their study of the cosmos. Professor Ward's erudition and spirit of grace played a crucial role in this part of the journey. Personally his own journey from avowed atheist to Faith acted as an inspiration.

Professor Mark Muesse, Professor of Religious Studies and Philosophy at Rhodes College in the USA, was to become one of my most beautiful guides. The luminosity of his spirit continues to lift me to this day. His insights to the Traditions of South Asia remain such a source of spiritual nourishment. Meeting him and his lovely family in London was one of the highlights of my life. His friendship and correspondence over the past several years was a source of knowledge and wisdom that has always been enveloped in love and light.

Father Ben O'Rourke, Augustinian scholar and one of the most love filled souls I have ever met, gave his time, guidance and compassion as my Faith found strength again. The time I spent with him in prayer and remembrance at Clare Priory in the English countryside shall live with me forever.

My meetings with Professor Mona Siddiqui and Reza Shah Kazemi were also blessings. For a number of their respective books had illuminated my understanding of the inner spirit of Faith, without which the outer rituals face the risk of being rendered arid and empty.

So many others whose work and lives are steeped in the spirituality of the heart gave their time generously. Such was the mercy of heaven that they helped this poor lost soul break free of the well into which I had fallen; their love and learning became the rope which pulled my heart out of darkness into light.

"I drenched my life with the works of Traditional Wisdom. I wrote to teachers whose works would help to restore my faith. And learned that this spirit of Traditional Wisdom continued to live….."

The Message of Eternity: Oneness

Oneness was the core perennial message that sounded in my soul as I consulted the founding and early texts and writers of Traditional Wisdom. How beautiful to see the praise of the One Source of all within the yearnings of the Sufi Mystics, the Desert Fathers and the Kabbalist's desire to become the embodiment of the *Shema*.

The mystics of these revelatory paths of Traditional Wisdom spoke the same language of love and of procession and return. When I shared, with friends, writings from each of these Traditions none could distinguish the "external" religion from which they emanated. All inner roads continue, as they have for millennia, to lead us to the same centre of but one circle.

It is worth re-iterating the core message of this perennial wisdom. For it posits that all Traditions should be seen as points on the circumference of a circle; such points representing the external (and contrasting) aspects of each Tradition. This wisdom asks us however to always keep remembering that the circle has but one centre point and leading to that centre are radii from each point on the circumference. These radii represent the mystical or inner path to the centre which is the same within each Tradition. For it requires the same purity of heart and has the same aspiration; a Union with that which is the First and the Last, the Outer and the Inner, the Source. The One.

All learning should be an act of transformation and self-improvement and self-realisation. For knowledge that does not lift us to our higher selves is but vain erudition.

This is a central truth of Traditional Wisdom. Ethics and integrity are the handmaidens of teacher and student and ascension to our highest selves is the ground within which all "acquisition" of learning is placed. That this seems so alien to the tenets of much of modern instruction in places of learning is perhaps a telling commentary on our times.

And so it proved that the very act of immersing myself in the teachings and teachers of Traditional Wisdom transformed me; it helped me recognise the illusions and veils of modernism. And lead to the realisation that the answers for which my heart yearned were here, within, all the time.

"The mystics of these revelatory paths of Traditional Wisdom spoke the same language of love and of procession and return. All inner roads continue, as they have for millennia, to lead us to the same centre of but one circle."

No longer need we pass over in silence that of which Modernism cannot speak; the sacred cosmology, ontology and anthropology which has for millennia been the very foundation of humanity. In Appendix 1 (at the end of this book) I have listed some of the key works that helped transform both my mind and heart toward that which is Eternal.

For now, I wish to share the larger themes of wisdom that all this journeying revealed; and how through wisdom's light my world, both within and without, was completely changed. Forever.

Sacred Cosmology: Procession and Return

From Him all proceeds and to Him all shall return. He is Love. Infinite and Wise. Majestic and Merciful. Beautiful and Powerful.

The One wished to be known and in the act of the greatest mercy and mystery Creation was initiated. That which was most Holy "became" first and, in a reflective act of continuous and infinite Love, emanation after emanation followed over aeons. With the remembrance always that those realms closest to the pristine purity of that first act of loving Self Disclosure reflect its beauty most faithfully.

With each level of Self Disclosure beauty and joy was brought into existence; each a reflection of the beauty and joy and love that preceded it.

From that First Unveiling the Heavenly Realms and Spiritual entities came into existence; each realm and each entity with a purpose to praise and glorify His Love. The

Angelic messengers tasked with the procession of all emanation so that even every drop of rain be accompanied on its path of supplication to the Source of all.

Such worlds contain the "signs" of heaven and lead to the final emanation which is our Created World. Between the higher Spiritual realms and this final physical realm lies a realm of the Imagination; not *imagined* (as in illusory) but rather an *Imaginal Realm* where the archetypes (cloaked in spiritual light) of the physical order reside. This *Imaginal Realm* also contains within its symbols and images the very language of the Heavenly Realms above. From which eternal Love, Truth and Beauty continually emanate.

The physical cosmos of our Universe has of course its own beauty; this must be praised even as, given its place in the hierarchy of emanation, its imperfection must be remembered.

All Creation, within our physical realm, is born anew in each moment. The One is busy on wondrous Self Disclosure on each "Day"; He resides in each epoch and He is the epoch we count in time and extension and space. Perpetual is His Love. Evidenced through this act of creation in each new moment. For even our next breath cannot be assured or be seen as our own but only as a gift from the Self-Disclosure of the Source of all. Each moment we are created once more; our tomorrow never the replica of our yesterday.

His love is both Transcendent and Immanent; utterly unreachable in its Essence yet closer to us than the very breath we take. That we may never know that Essence is an acceptance and surrender that is a source of our mystery and strength. Perhaps only by saying what He is *not* can we even glimpse that eternal "no-thingness" which even the most beautiful expressions of our language cannot approach let alone describe.

"All Creation, within our physical realm, is born anew in each moment. Each moment we are created once more; our tomorrow never the replica of our yesterday."

Sacred Ontology: Being and Knowing

All that proceeds and returns is but one. All is a mirror giving the reflection of the Real. The One.

There is multiplicity when we look around us in the created realm; there is multiplicity in the many heavens whose angelic and other beings carry out the work as His messengers.

Yet each is but part of His Being; our being too is but a reflection of that Oneness of Being. Such a sacred "Ontology" (theory of being) is one of Unity. All emanations united in their origin and return.

Our being subsides within the Infinite. Our creation a forbear of Time and Space. In His Self-Disclosure we were born and remain love itself. Thus our being and existence is spiritual in its essence and preceded the physical universe which acts as a theatre into which our lives are manifest. Our existence did not commence when we received the garments we call our bodies. They are our garments in the created realm which we shall shed as we journey home. That home which we knew when the Breath of Heaven filled out spirit.

"Our being and existence is spiritual in its essence and preceded the physical universe which acts as a theatre into which our lives are manifest"

He is the First and the Last. The outer and inner. The exoteric and esoteric.

All creation contains His "signs" and each contains many levels of meaning. The created order, the cosmos, nature, the multiplicity of beings are all potential gates to the Divine or veils that keep us in the shadows. Depending on the orientation and purity of our heart.

Yet if we can see beyond the surface and recall the Source of All we can truly have an epistemology (theory of knowledge) that can see the Unity and Oneness at the heart of all truth. For all knowledge is but an encounter or embrace with the Real. That Divine Reality who shares His Love in Infinite and multiple acts of creation while His Oneness remains complete in its perfect simplicity and ceaseless beauty.

Sacred Anthropology: The Heritage of Humanity

The breath of the Divine, through the conduit of Eternal Wisdom, brought humanity into being as part of its Being. Ours is the privilege to be the servant and representative of heaven in the final emanation of the Divine, the Physical world we occupy.

Long ago we entered into an eternal covenant before our world was brought into existence. When we were told the sacred name (or essence) of all that would exist in this physical realm. To us bowed the angels and the creatures who would become our brethren in this cycle of time. Though they feared the blood we would spill the One assured them that He knew what they did not.

In our perfected state we, humanity, encompass all the created world. For this covenant gives us trusteeship of its passage in linear time. We are the microcosm to its macrocosm. As we align and lift ourselves to our highest self we lift the world and its existence to its highest manifestation. Every action, inaction, intention, feeling, desire, want, yearning we permit to enter our heart creates or destroys the world we see around us.

Our sacred anthropology tells us we exist in societies each of which, through all human time, has been sent a messenger. Each messenger the conveyer of but the same essential message; Oneness.

Our sacred psychology asks us to pit our Light or Spiritual Essence against the demands of our lower soul or ego which draws us toward the ephemeral and transient. The lower soul is allured by the treasures of this world. Ardent in its desire to satiate that which can never be satisfied. Our Light or Spiritual Essence is the source of the Divine breath and only through its honouring can we have any hope to redeem the pledge of the covenant we made long years ago.

Our body is the conveyance for this period of earthly time and to the extent we can have the courage, to love and wage spiritual war upon our lower soul, shall our body thrive and its beauty be truly manifested. Who can fail to see the luminous beauty in the countenance of one whose heart is bathed in the Light of Heavenly love?

For He So Loved to be known that He created us in his Image and Form. We must not chastise our body for it is but He who has bequeathed it to us. So that it may help us to carry out the awesome covenantal responsibility we bear in this created realm.

We must not even chastise our lower soul for in it we are asked to choose the higher over the lower, the light over the darkness and unity over division. In this dualistic dance we shall find our courage and triumph over the temporal.

For the heart of humanity is one of the three "books" in which Heaven conveys its messages; the others being the "book" of Sacred Scripture and the "book" of Nature with which we are surrounded during our time on earth.

By journeying within we can use our light to understand the

message of heaven. And through this "inner vision" of the heart we can learn the language of the Divine; to see through the veils of the created order. For via this "sight" we reveal an isthmus, and can stand in that *Imaginal realm* which contains the symbols of Heaven's intent. That intermediate realm between the physical and purely spiritual.

In this way we may hope, to once again, know the sacred names or Essence of all forms; each creation having both an outer or exterior aspect and most importantly an inner essence which is the reflection of its archetype in the Imaginal realm.

By our Light within our heart we can once again be awakened to who we truly are, and to know from where we have come, and to where we are ultimately destined to return.

"Every action, inaction, intention, feeling, desire, want, yearning we permit to enter our heart creates or destroys the world we see around us."

One Light: one heart

For the truth of Oneness means the sacred cosmology reveals what is truly real (metaphysics); and sacred ontology tells us our being is within His Being and that therefore we can know (epistemology)the Truth of Oneness as our own Light is but an emanation of it.

Our sacred psychology and anthropology guides us to know the inner meaning of the three "books" through which Heaven has conveyed the meaning of its messages. The book of Nature, the sacred book of scripture and the book contained within our heart.

Ultimately when we can read the "book "of our sacred human nature we have finally possession of the key to lead us out of the cage of the created order. For the Light within is contained in our heart; and the heart is the centre of each of us. And it too, for those that have truly surrendered to Heaven's Traditional Wisdom, is the centre of the Universe. For the Universe was not something into which we were plunged but rather it was created and grounded within the Divine spark that has always been and shall remain our essence.

And so months after I fell into even greater despair as I tried to find answers within the "knowledge" of modernism (so much of which is but a veil) I found that it was within Traditional Wisdom that my salvation had come and within which it would abide.

Faith is no caravan of despair. For the call of Heaven, akin to its acts of creation, is perpetual. Come, come, come again heaven implores. Come back to your true home and true nature.

For there is but one Light. One source. And by looking up and within we can follow the path from darkness to Light.

For ultimately there is only unity. Knower and known are one. Subject and object are one. We are the Light. And its Language of Love resides within our heart.

And it is now to the central importance of that receptacle, our heart, and the need to ensure it is sufficiently purified, that we turn. And undertake the first three steps of our Spiritual Solution.

THE PATH OF KNOWLEDGE

Chapter 6: The Treasure of Healing

Spiritual Solution: Steps 1-3

__Summary:__ When we understand how the modern worldview has denied the Truth of Traditional Wisdom we begin to see that this betrayal underlies many of the ills within our hearts and that which we witness in the world around us. Reclaiming a sacred worldview which the ancients and the greatest amongst us have revealed rents asunder many of the veils clouding the Light within our heart.
When we learn to "look up" (step 1), "look around" (step 2) and finally "look within" (step 3) we transform our existence. And this inevitably leads to the power of prayer re-emerging in our daily life.

Traditional Wisdom had now restored a radically different way to understand existence, being and humanity. It seemed (at times) a long and arduous journey to find my way toward and absorb the insights of Traditional Wisdom. For throughout the process the voice within continued to pour doubt on the openings that my heart was experiencing.

From the absolute certainty of the world(s)-view offered by Traditional Wisdom – and recognition of what we had lost or discarded during the move to Modernism-I was able to make sense of the steps that presented themselves to me as crucial to my return to the Spirit.

The Spiritual Solution-Step 1: *Look up- cosmology and metaphysics*

The recovering of Traditional Wisdom pierced the veil of modernism's closing of the heavenly realm. It allowed me to see the hierarchy that the ancients had made the pole around which their lives were orientated. I was able to access a cosmology (theory of the created order) and a metaphysics (that which is truly Real) that radiated far beyond the material realm.

The greatest of those who have travelled this Earth before us left us clues to find the peace that is our heritage; they suffered so that perhaps we may suffer less. And if suffering is to be part of our path (which in this imperfect realm it must needs be) let us embrace that suffering as a symbol that we are remembered by the One who orders all.

My healing truly began, my search for meaning truly began, my walk from being a servant to my shadows, to being a servant to the Light began with this first step. Looking up and seeing the world through the eyes of Wisdom.

I looked up with the eyes of my heart. I saw for the first time in decades (and perhaps for the first time with certainty) the symbols and "signs" that the Heavens continually reveal: to guide those who are journeying back to their true home.

"My healing truly began, my search for meaning truly began, my walk from being a servant to my shadows, to being a servant to the Light began with this first step."

When you see that there is a centre point or Source from which all proceeds and to which all must eventually return, there is discovered a strength in our surrender and valour in our vulnerability.

Whilst the Essence of the One may never be known to us, Traditional Wisdom informed me that He was closer to me than the veins in my heart. His Transcendence and Immanence (or manifestation in all), assured me that my pleas for guidance and help were never failing to be heard.

When we see that the Source of all was a Hidden Treasure who in an act of the most supreme love wanted to be known and created all the levels of reality from the highest to the lowest; with that vision we become not solitary brutish or purposeless but divine sparks whose very existence makes the world.

The inevitable result of knowing that creation came from an act of Supreme Love and that there was indeed an infinite realm or number of realms beyond that defined by modernism was that awe and yearning flooded my heart.

This helped to drive out fear and pain. When we shrink with misapprehension we cut off what is boundless and replace it with that which is confining and binding to our self.

One day I heard the voice within guide me (for the first time in more years than I can remember) to turn to prayer. With the remembrance that true prayer was not mere formulaic observance. The exterior actions of Prayer (posture, breathing and supplication) always pointed to an esoteric or inner significance. To an orientation of joyful surrender and Faith in the Infinite.

My true prayer began with the intention in my heart. I stepped out of the liner time and space which I occupy here in my body; a means of shutting the world out and its infinite demands and claims on our time, emotions and energy, is that prize which Traditional Wisdom offers through prayer.

The purpose of prayer includes its role as a means for our protection. As a shield to let flourish the beauty of the light within; outside we may strive for fortune and fame and they never prove lasting panaceas for our deepest desire. That desire for love, to be loved and express love.

So I had to re-learn the way to pray; initially it was just falling onto my knees and offering up my soul for communion with the Presence that is always present. The Presence whose closeness to our heart is attested in all Traditional Wisdom. Whose companionship is available in every moment.

"The exterior actions of Prayer (posture, breathing and supplication) always pointed to an esoteric or inner significance. To an orientation of joyful surrender and Faith in the Infinite."

Eventually and fighting the habits of distraction (there is always an excuse to find to justify completing that one task, making that one phone call or sending that one vital text or email) I made prayer the core part of my daily life. Punctuated by prayer my day now offered moments- even in the midst of frenetic activity, travel or the traffic of London! - of peace and healing that rejuvenated my soul. A source of priceless enrichment.

This step is a dynamic one for my prayers continue each day and every day. They are the cardinal points around which all endeavours and actions of daily life are orientated.

Whatever the distinctions within the canonical prayers of the various Traditions they all offer a path to guide us home; to the Light in heaven and the Light within our heart. Prayer reminds us, through the warmth with which it envelops us, that this Light is but the same.

Spiritual Solution- Step 2: look around- Ontology and epistemology

Traditional Wisdom in much if not most of its teachings sees us as individuals within communities or nations or tribes and further as part of a created order redolent with the "signs" of heaven.

The nature of our existence/being ("ontology") carries the paradox of our absolute no-thingness before Ultimate Transcendence and our central role in the drama of the continuous self-manifestation of the Hidden Treasure of Divine Beauty.

The Hand that created all of the Created Order (and indeed all realms) through Its emptying of Itself left its Divine Light in every blade of grass and in the breath of every animal.

This step made the world around come alive and my heart saw "signs" of the language of Heaven in all things; love. Each stone, each tree, each bird, each mammal, each creature of the sea; they are in submission to the Hand that created them, the very same that created us. They offer their own means of glorifying Heaven though we may never have the privilege to hear them; for if we could we too may be able to submit in love as fully as they do and know our highest peace. Condemned to be "free", however, we must seek the middle path, between faithful surrender and hubristic rebellion, as our anthropology demands.

"This step made the world around come alive and my heart saw "signs" of the language of Heaven in all things; love."

There are, as we saw in the previous chapter, also those "signs" and symbols within the *Imaginal* Realm. This realm and its symbols contains the messages of the Heavenly realm which are always unveiling their inner meaning. Through the purity of our heart we have unique (amongst the creatures of creation) access to this realm if we can take the time to strive to hear its call.

For me this meant greater commitment to remain immersed within each moment; rather than looking ahead or worrying about that which had passed. It meant finding time to walk in any manifestation of nature (even within the small haven of a city park) when I was otherwise surrounded by the grey and grind of daily commuters and workers.

It also meant that I used time to have compassion for our brethren in the animal kingdom whose suffering could not any longer easily be excluded, consciously or otherwise, from my consciousness. When we see all is connected we cannot construct fences to flee from the fate of others. Such a sense of oneness and connectedness is wonderful though it offers its insights not without demands. For the price we shall pay for such insights is the pain in our heart; that must come when we awaken to the imperfections and conflicts that are an inevitable part of the created order.

Would that we can, each and all of us, take the leap and change our world completely. So that it could reflect the light we all share. And attain that professed vision that could make the world the place we all seek; Would that we could live in harmony to use the precious and sacred "resources" of the world- which in truth are our brothers and sisters including the most basic of the elements to the most sophisticated of animals- in ways that honour the kindred origins of all.

Until that time, which Traditional Wisdom teaches must come (though it keeps its own counsel about the hour of its unveiling) what are we to do?

When we "see" with our heart that tragedy which is unfolding around us; to Mother Earth in her unadorned core beauty?

We can perhaps take a first step; a small step; incrementally remove the barriers and veils that permit us to see only the externals of creation. Even as there shall be those amongst us who are tasked by Providence to be the iconoclasts of this Age; who stridently promote, through their personal example and their convictions, the welfare of all our fellow creation. Theirs is the blessing and responsibility of Heaven; to be lauded and followed as best as we can.

Specifically, for me this meant changing my relationship within my heart to flora and fauna. To treat with the deepest respect, the petals of each flower and opening my heart with love to the variegated forms found in creation. I still recall for example the occasions when (following torrential showers) my young daughter and I walked along the pavements outside our home to gently collect the snails that had come out from under their shelters. For they were now exposed on the busy pavements and the deadly roads. Our returning them to safety away from danger was one of the beautiful moments she and I have shared.

Natural too now is the prayer I utter whenever I see the body of an animal whose light has returned to the Source of all; the same prayer that my daughter and I say when conducting a burial ceremony for the mice that our cats present to us as "gifts" from time to time. Effortless now also seems the greetings of peace and blessings that I give to as many animals that cross my path and consciousness each day. History gives us many inspiring exemplars of the saintliness of communing with Heaven's creatures.

In such supplications I am each moment honouring the sacred *Ontology* (the nature of Being) of my kindred in creation. In that honouring I am bestowed with deeper knowledge of the connectedness of all; this theory of knowledge (epistemology)is founded not simply on what we can *rationally* know but on what our hearts *experience* as truth through the principle of Oneness. Manifested most fruitfully through the love in our hearts.

"For the price we shall pay for such insights is the pain in our heart; that must come when we awaken to the imperfections and conflicts that are an inevitable part of the created order."

Perhaps my greatest prayer would be that long after I have left this created realm my daughter may recall these joint spiritual exercises and that she will have the opportunity to pass this Oneness and love for all to her own children. And for her to know that in that compassion for all resides the true nature of authentic self-love.

Spiritual Solution-Step 3: look within – anthropology and ethics

Many of our most treasured stories and cultural legends invite us to marvel at the journeys that those who are heroic must undertake, in order to complete the mission burning in their hearts.

The first two steps ("looking up" and "looking within") to my healing represented the journey I had to make up toward the Heavens; one that had to be draped in awe and yearning. I also had to make the journey around me in order to see the "signs" representing Heaven's sacred revealing.

"Journeying within is the path that perhaps more than any other opened the vessels of my heart."

Yet all roads lead us home. Our return is a journey we must make within, while our Spirit and Light occupies our physical body. Journeying within is the path that perhaps more than any other opened the vessels of my heart. Only through such openings can we receive and emit the Light of love in each day, each hour and even each moment. It was when I permitted the exterior to be bathed by that which burns so brightly within, that true transformation was possible.

Traditional Wisdom had taught me to discard that profanity that pervades popular paradigms; that we are accidental by products of merciless forces originating in a vacuum and leading purposelessly and pitilessly to a future ultimately as uncertain as it is lifeless. Death of self. Death of Mother Earth. Death of the Universe. No beyond. Finality.

As we have seen Traditional Wisdom instead sees humanity as the bearers of the most majestic of the attributes of the Divine Beauty. My journey within, through these frames of reference, lead to an ocean of potentiality that existed in my heart.

Yet the journey to that ocean without a shore commenced by having to confront the darkness of my soul; for Man carries a call to ascension within his soul if he is to have any hope to be bathed by the beatitude of the Light that resides in his heart.

Our lower soul is the seat of our greatest battle; far greater than the external battles or wars that we in our individuality (or indeed as a collectivity) have to face. Until we have triumphed in the battlefield within our breast we are destined to repeat the mistakes of our history. One so dominated by the covetousness whose genesis is found in the lower soul; whose voice speaks its ceaseless demands each day.

It is perhaps for only the saints and seers to conquer

completely this lower soul; the one whose entreaties call for our reducing our actions and aspirations to the simple fulfilment of its wishes. Impossible to satiate its demands, when we let it become our master, we fall into a bondage from which we may truly never escape. For its familiarity acts as a blindfold to the vision within.

"Until we have triumphed in the battlefield within our breast we are destined to repeat the mistakes of our history."

From one who was so enslaved I can attest to the destructive price that such a master exacts on our heart. Whatever the accoutrements, in our zest for our lower soul's satiation, we may have acquired, often it is too late before we realise that their value is rendered a nullity. When placed in comparison to what we have sacrificed for their acquisition.

Yet even if we are never destined to be saints or seers surely their example can serve as a guide to the mastery of this "traitor" in our midst?

The first step is always knowledge and recognition; of the true nature of who we are. For ours is a sacred anthropology. It's message the very opposite of modernism's view of humanity. For the Sacred teaches that we are Divine Lights into whom the breath of compassion was given; so that we could carry the essential message of heaven to all here in this finite realm. That covenant was consecrated before Time and Space became categories of creation and our pledge was recorded. Such pledge was entered into before the witness of all the flora and fauna that were to become our companions in this cycle of existence.

We shall redeem that pledge and honour the covenant whose wisdom is our heritage only by extinguishing the darkness within our lower soul. Our weapon in this fight lies in the radiance of the Light shining in our heart.

After recognising the workings and whispering of the lower soul it is to the power of prayer and the remembrance of the Divine to which we must turn. For each are arrows of Truth to lay bare the paucity of promises offered by the lower part of our soul.

Years had passed since I had offer prayers with faith-filled purpose. Shame and self-effacement notwithstanding I brushed off this lack of familiarity and began to make prayer a permanent feature of my life. This was formal "canonical" prayer which eventually over time (would that I could have adopted this practice immediately) punctuated my life throughout each day. Such prayer acts as a fisherman's net bringing its catch into certainty and preventing one's drowning in the waves of the ephemeral.

As prayer became a haven of escape I added the remembrance of the Divine Name within my daily routine. Simply a few minutes of silent sitting and sometimes contemplation of the Name of the One; at other times whispered recitals of the Name acted as balm to my heart. I would sit in my car between meetings or dive into a place of worship in London's frenetic centre and find time for this sacred offering of myself to the Highest Light.

Nothing is without consequences. The cosmic law of justice assures us of this truth; even if many times we cannot discern its exquisite operation, given the finitude of our perception and the span of our earthly existence.

Perhaps the greatest consequence from the ability to finally "look within" was the recognition of the sacrality of a timeless ethics. A set of values that carry the weight of the Divine emptying into the created order. That means that we, each one of us, make or break the world with every action, every intent and perhaps even every thought.

Values rooted in Traditional Wisdom are not based on a calculus of utility or expediency; they are not to be subsumed in the momentary lapse of a collective into an abyss of darkness. Instead they stand transcendent to any fashion, political or intellectual, that dominates any contingent and ephemeral passage of our history.

Integrity, honour, truth, justice, fidelity, respect, compassion, courage, fortitude, fairness, piety, humility, service, charity, hope, faith, mercy, and Love. These are the "icons" of the Divine; when we understand that any "icon" must point to a Truth beyond itself. Such values centre our soul in the path where it can truly express its primordial nature.

Rooted firmly within the tree of wisdom that Tradition plants via Divine Grace these values are the ones which reveal the truth of our intent. Their presence or absence attest to whether we have chosen the path that accords with the highest within us or otherwise. In that moment when we dilute their purity and pristine beauty we begin to denude the perfection that resides in our heart.

We who have surely played the rhetorician's game (and sought to find pretext for the actions which our heart always knew compromised any of these values) have to confront the realisation that we are the authors of our destiny. That this is the foundation of freewill that was a "prize" we have been bequeathed. The prize which permits us to lift ourselves to angel ship or descend to that which is most loathsome in our tendencies.

"I can speak as one who blighted his existence for years in the shadowy compromises which characterise so much of the relativity which lies in the bosom of modernism."

But our cosmology precedes our ontology which grounds our Anthropology. Our humanity cannot be understood outside the nature of our being (as creations of the Divine) which is part of a vast hierarchy that passes through all the emanations that proceed from the Source of all. The fullness of the Divine Centre is such that its infinite love and compassion permeates all levels of existence in the hierarchy of creation.

Any Ethics grounded in this Divine flow of unending Love

and Mercy simply cannot be contingent. Set aloft by the Absolute the values encompassed by sacred ethics protect and promote our desire to do that which is beautiful; that to which our heart strives.

These values become the prism through which we see the world and the choices that confront us in every moment (whether routine or seminal) of our life.

I can speak as one who blighted his existence for years in the shadowy compromises which characterise so much of the relativity which lies in the bosom of modernism. The price of such a calamitous calculus manifested in the aloneness gripping my heart even when all the allures of the world swirled around.

Now years after the commencement of my spiritual journey can I, at last, attest that that which had enslaved me has become anathema even to my thoughts; no longer do the "paths of least resistance" hold their appeal. I shall not miss their absence from my life.

The process of "looking within" and understanding my place in the cosmos has done much more than simply act as a mechanism to repress the ardent addictions of amorality. The purifying effect of this stage of the path of knowledge has virtually extinguished even the propensity to consider the temptations that had formerly been the source of my weakness for decades.

Unifying the act of surrender involved in "looking up, around and within" has been the reclamation of the centrality of prayer in my daily life. Food and sustenance I can afford to deprive myself of; this cannot be said of the practice of prayer which permeates my personal journey as never before. Aligned with the remembrance of the Divine this ever more optimally ensures that my very *mode of being* is a reflection of the primordial light. That which illumines my path from this world to the worlds that all inner ascension must surely lead toward.

The Path of Action
Chapter 7: Polishing our heart

The Spiritual Solution: Steps 4 and 5
Summary: The "path of knowledge" opens our heart to wisdom. Now it is the heart that will need purification in order to have sufficient receptivity to the Light of Heaven. The process of purification requires that we confront our lives (step 4) fully and stand witness to all we have done. We must then proceed to offer contrition (step 5) to our confession so that we remove any opaqueness within the mirror within which our inner light is housed.

The path of knowledge had cleared the fog that had acted as a blinding force preventing me from seeing the wisdom of the ages that was always present under my very gaze. I was now orientated with the sight of the "eye of the heart"; that sight which need not seek the goodwill of authority in order to express its authenticity.

There was liberation in recognising our being as rooted in the cosmology that offers ascension in endless beauty and placed our hearts in the centre of the universe. Perhaps when an ancient wisdom spoke of the geocentric heavens it meant that it was the human heart which was the symbolic centre for all the created order. For if we are indeed the microcosm as the universe is the macrocosm then through our actions all energy proceeds and returns to the fount of love in our heart.

"There remains however a chasm between the illumination of knowledge and the steps to be taken in the light of that new vision; for action must ensue from the receptacle that fuels the fire of Faith in Traditional Wisdom. That receptacle is the heart"

Conferred with this new vision of "being" meant all of nature speaks to us; each day. Of its sorrows and triumphs and its surrender to our stewardship, even as it beseeches us to remember the oneness that is the organising principle of all.

Prayer offered me the ladder of ascension. In order to see life from a new vantage point; from up there and not from down here. To the extent that we arrive at the place of supplication cleansed of our distractions and desires, only then do we reflect the grace that permeates the sacredness of such communion with heaven.

Knowledge must transform and this must be evidenced in the actions that then dominate our lives; a knowledge or philosophy that does not cause such transformation is a vainglorious deceit. An inflation of the ego and honouring of that tendency to hubris that marks the worst of those who have fallen prey to the project of the deification of man.

Crossing the bridge to action

There remains however a chasm between the illumination of knowledge and the steps to be taken in the light of that new vision; for action must ensue from the receptacle that fuels the fire of Faith in Traditional Wisdom. That receptacle is the heart; not the physical organ of biology but the true centre of our being (our ontological essence) which is the guardian of the Light of Heaven.

Until this receptacle is fit for the purpose of spiritual renewal we shall face inertia in our yearning to transform our behaviour in life. Traditional Wisdom teaches that this receptacle is akin to a lamp within which our light is housed. Yet the lamp over time may have become opaque through the dust accumulated from the karmic consequences of our time in the wilderness of wasteful endeavours.

The turn to Traditional wisdom's teaching in the "path of knowledge" – and the rejection of the world turned inside out by modernism- had by this time served to begin the polishing of the lamp of my heart. All that we experience shall become part of ourselves and the drenching of my mind, body and spirit in the Traditional texts had already begun the cleansing of this lamp of light.

To Providence I remain indebted for it is was at this time, perhaps a couple of years into my journey, that the second of the three "calamities" (I referred to in chapter 2) befell me.

As the battle raged within between my lower soul that dominates so much of our thinking and the purifying waters of Divine Wisdom, I found once again I came to very familiar crossroads; those that confront us so often when we have the choice between descent into the "path of least resistance" (whatever that may be for us) and the prospective ascent to actualise our potentiality to reflect the Divine.

Rarely is the transformative journey of those that seek the return to Source a straight line that seamlessly takes us to the summit of the ladder of ascension; often we will trip and lose our balance and orientation. Perhaps each step requires all our concentration or we shall be required to begin the ascent again from the lowest rung.

This second "calamity" took place in late 2014 and suddenly and without warning lead to the complete collapse of my business endeavours; the financial pressures that this brought were acute and yet more damaging was the destructive effect on my spirit within the world of business. So much value we attach to the status and signification that comes from "success" in the world that we overlook how ephemeral even these icons are in our lives.

From the perspective of time I can now see that this occurred at precisely the perfect moment as the pretence of my personality was erased and exposed. Should we endow externals with so much existential value in our lives? My heart knew that indeed it was folly to do so, as the fall from grace in those weeks following the business collapse, shattered the illusions that I now learned were still part of the way I looked at the world.

Through this event I was guided to strip away these last vestiges of illusion from my self-reflection and begin the necessary task of polishing the mirror of my Being.

This took me to the next three steps, all within the Path of Action, of the journey that had at that stage been grounded on the path of knowledge.

These three steps comprised the continuum of confession, contrition and finally the cleansing balm of forgiveness.

Spiritual Solution- Step 4 (Self Truth; Confession)

During a recent summer visit to Andalusia (absolutely my favourite part of the world) I was tasked to repaint and transform a heavy wooden front door.

Before the new coat of varnish could be applied (and which would undoubtedly offer a brilliant fresh and wonderful appearance to the entrance to the house) there was a need to undertake the hard and laborious task of removing the existing worn varnish. Furthermore, the door would also need to be sanded very carefully and extensively to remove the imperfections that had gathered within the grain of the wood over the years.

As we travel from the foundation of freedom offered by the *path of knowledge* to the *path of action* and ultimately the *path of love* we too need to remove our spirit's coat of varnish which we may have permitted to lose its lustre. We also need to identify and remove the imperfections and faults that have become part of the fabric of our being over the years.

It is hard work. Repetitive and painful both in the physical sense of the varnishing of the door in the example above and also spiritually and emotionally as we seek to emulate the desire to be transfigured by the light in our heart. So that this receptacle of our Divine light, our heart, can become once again fit for the purpose for which Infinite Intelligence brought it into being. To love, to grow, to know and ultimately to seek union with our true home.

"Yet my heart continued to draw me to that path I had taken years before. Toward the light, promised in the texts of Traditional Wisdom, that simultaneously resided in heaven and within each of us."

Many are the lies that we seek to either avoid confronting or we even construct in our efforts to make palatable the choices we know are confected from the false promises of the ephemeral.

Until we confront and lay bare these lies our path to the transformation we so ardently seek shall be made impassable by that densest of forests; self-deceit. The darkness of our heart creates the deepest roots in the soil of our souls nourished by every incremental self-deceit we perpetrate.

My spiritual journey continued even amidst the chaos and confusion wrought by the failure in my business life; haunted I became with inner images of disappointment. Yet my heart continued to draw me to that path I had taken years before. Toward the light (promised in the texts of Traditional Wisdom) that simultaneously resided in heaven and within each of us.
So I stood before the mirror of true self-reflection. My memories were stirred and I recalled how, many times before, I had come to stand before the very same mirror of true self- reflection.
I recalled being in Ecuador to attend one of my dearest and closest friend's weddings; I had fallen to my knees as my

efforts to hold back the tears from so many unfulfilled years had failed. And I recall the promises I made then to reclaim the path to the Spirit; and how empty those "promises" had proved to be in the decade or so since that anguished hour.

Yet the mercy of Heaven is limitless and now here I was again before that same inner mirror. Which as ever faithfully was reflecting back to me that which was the true nature of what I had become. Would courage fail me once again? Would I dishonour the truths I had now installed within my heart? Would I turn away again from the pain of memory? Would I be prepared to confess and bear my own passion? Would I be able to stand in my aloneness before the Most Merciful whose Grace never ends? Would I see this as another crossroads from which to flee to comfort?

By whatever instrument we are guided in our most crucial moments we must give thanks; for its operation is surely in the gift of the Source of all. Whose recognition of the soul that is truly yearning for redemption is reciprocated in ceaseless compassion.

And so this time I did not permit courage to collapse. I did not avert my gaze from the reflections revealed in the mirror of my mind. I knew it was the time to confront the shadows we all hide within. Many if not most of mine I had authored through my own actions. So I stood before the mirror and did not flinch.

This was not a single exercise of course; there was so much to confess that I would have had to abjure all the demands of my body had I sought to erase, in one sitting, all the shadows whose demands I now had to acknowledge and ultimately reject.

Over a period of time I spent time – dedicated time- to play "the film" of my life. I went through all the actions, inactions and the intentions (honourable or otherwise) that gave birth to them. It is said that at the end of life we will either reflect on the journey with pride or regret; that our lives will either be an example or a warning.

Fortunately, each moment is the rebirth of ourselves and the universe anew; that next moment can truly lead to the catalyst that creates a new destiny. Provided we are not closed to the awesome power of Grace that is with us from cradle to the grave.

"By whatever instrument we are guided in our most crucial moments we must give thanks; for its operation is surely in the gift of the Source of all. Whose recognition of the soul that is truly yearning for redemption is reciprocated in ceaseless compassion."

Please let no one deceive us that this step- of confession and witness to our deepest selves-is easy or one which we can traverse without being utterly changed. The step is only valid if we hold back nothing from our gaze; we have to embrace with all our passion the fear that resides within us until it subsides and is subsumed in the light of love in our heart.

This requires Faith. Not a glib formulaic expression of Faith or mechanical mantra. Neither of which will offer us protection in what shall surely be the most violent of storms within our consciousness.

No. It requires that we are indeed seeing the world with the *mode of being* that is orientated to the cosmology, ontology and anthropology offered by Traditional Wisdom. Then and only then will we recognise the full panoply of enticements offered by our lower ego. Those familiar enticements that the lower ego will offer us in its prideful haste, to shield us from the Truth we know we must hear if we are to heal and be transformed.

Hence the perhaps disproportionate time we have spent in the section on "the path of knowledge" for it is the foundation for the new temple we must create within our hearts. One that honours who we are and is strong enough to withstand the winds of change we must welcome to clear the debris we have collected in our living years.

So I allowed myself to "re-live" all the times and episodes- many which had resided deep in the recesses of memory for so long- of which I was ashamed; those where I had sold the pristine preciousness of my soul for the lowest of prices. This was in full and brilliant resolution not grainy shadowy images; nothing was left out of the picture.

I recalled also the intentions and the state of my soul during each of these episodes and events; they revealed a heart that was indeed turned inside out. A heart which was the exact opposite to the heroic endeavours for which we have each been created. I often found myself shivering in the shadow of so many shattered expectations. Yet sometimes it is only when we see the emptiness of the life we have lived that we can recognise the warmth offered by the eternal light within. That light which is present always to offer the way to soothe our pain.

Remembrance of all the aspirations that I had had held so dear in my formative years brought perhaps the most desolation to my heart. I now know the truth of what I had permitted to unfold in my life; and more accurately I knew the truth of the illusory and ephemeral to which I had not simply acquiesced but to which I had fled with the worst of passionate conviction.

The faces and souls of those I had let down were like the ghosts of fairy tales that haunted me in the depths of my slumber at night. And also in those moments during the day when we find our inner gaze drifting to the lands occupied by our memory.

All of the above involved unflinching honesty and the deadliest of details to be unearthed. Such witness took time and was very much a personal journey I took when alone; often deep into the night when the quiet acted as an invitation to be fulsome in my witness.

"So I allowed myself to "re-live" all the times and episodes of which I was ashamed; those where I had sold the pristine preciousness of my soul for the lowest of prices."

I also undertook the witnessing in the presence of one of the teachers to whom I had been guided by the Mercy of Heaven. This was the wonderful Father Ben O'Rourke whose beautiful book (The Hidden Treasure) is a must for anyone seeking to find the peace within their heart.

I made the journey to see Father Ben after having read his book and his companionship provided a wonderful fountain of love from which to draw as I completed the three steps in the path of action. This path began with the witness and confession I have outlined above.

Spiritual Solution- Step 5: Contrition

Let us return to our analogy of re-varnishing the door. The act of confession we have just covered in step 4, may be akin to being part of the preparation required before we can apply the new coat of varnish.

The remaining part of the preparation required me to move from confession to contrition.

Invitations adorn our popular media and culture asking us to embrace all that we have gone through to reach where we are at this present moment. Inviting us further to see all the faults and the wrong turns we have taken as pieces of the jigsaw that reveal the image of who we are. We are asked to accept all such actions yet often not offer penitence for them.

Seductive is the allure of such a precept; and indeed at a transcendent level there is an imperative surely to see every event, every action, every decision, every defeat and victory as part of a rich tapestry whose artistry is testimony to the Greatest Artist of all.

Yet we must be cautious to elide remembrance into acceptance. Somewhere deep inside, our heart will bear the wounds of all those whose lives we have diminished; whether unintentionally, indifferently or (most heinously) deliberately. All those with whom we have spent time on our journeying even if for the briefest of times.

Sorrow has a place at the table of our highest emotions; at the table of our manifestation of the highest within us.

Proverbial now is the admonition that sorry can indeed be the hardest word. Yet without heartfelt sorrow can we truly witness our confession? Will the testimony of our witnessing be accepted at the end of times when all that has unfolded shall be brought to account?

These questions had only one answer. Absence sorrow our job of work would be incomplete. Akin to removing the old coat of varnish from the door, yet neglecting to undertake the sacrifice required to sand away the imperfections and indentations that had accumulated over the years of exposure to life.

Accordingly, to my heart I ventured and opened its doors fully. With all my sincerity (evidenced by the tears and supplications rendered to heaven) I offered apology for my manifold failings. To heaven certainly for only it alone can truly by Grace make us be born anew in our heart. To those also to whom my impact had been diminishing (and no doubt in some cases damaging) I begged forgiveness. In my Imagination I visualised meeting with them and asking for their acknowledgment of the sincerity of my sorrow.

"Yet we must be cautious to elide remembrance into acceptance. Somewhere deep inside, our heart will bear the wounds of all those whose lives we have diminished"

Abject are we when we brush aside those whose souls we have darkened in the desire to escape the responsibility of true confession. Fortunately, time has however revealed that this was not to be my moment of cowardice. Not in this moment of renewal and authenticity. Regret would no longer be a burden that I was forced to carry into the future for failings in the present.

So I continued. In solitude, sometimes in silence and always in sincerity, I went through it all; the entire gallery of events that had each contributed to the darkness in my soul. So much I had lost along the away and to think I was the author of so much from which I had sought refuge. Repentance was my road to the riches of renewal.

In addition to this individual act of continual repentance- for long were the weeks and months to which I devoted to this crucial step in completing the confession I had already made- I also sat, as mentioned above, in the humbling presence of Father Ben O'Rourke. His guidance reinforced the message that in a single act of true repentance we can indeed enter into the bosom of Heaven anew. In one of the most beautiful memories of my life Father Ben and I shared laughter (and a few tears) as we spent precious time together; his scholarship and the Holy Presence that he exuded made me truly grateful that he would embrace one such as me.

Here we were brothers in Faith. Together recounting the blessings of Traditional Wisdom. Even as, in the outside world, the forces that promote division, hate and denigration of "the Other" found ever more free expression of their dangerous desire to engender a clash of civilisations.

I should add that, in my confession and contrition with Father Ben, I spoke of only generalities in contrast with the specificity of my supplications when taking steps 4 and 5 in solitude.

Traditional wisdom enjoins that once we have confessed and made complete that confession (with the contrition that wells from the depths of our soul) then we can close the door to the shadows of the past. They no longer need to blight our presence or diminish the light into which we have stepped.

Eschew we must the constant remembrance of the wrongs that we have perpetrated; not in order to render them unimportant for they each carry cosmic consequences, the result of which can only be fully revealed to us at the cessation of this cycle of Time and Space.

Rather we must recognise the power that they once exercised over us and which still resides latent within their recollection. We would have only raced to their allure, in the first instance, for the benefit that they bestowed to our lower soul; transient and ephemeral though such benefit surely was, we cannot overlook the potency (in recalling these episodes) to prevent our true cleansing within.

"Traditional wisdom enjoins that once we have confessed and made complete that confession then we can close the door to the shadows of the past."

And so gratefully and with a sense peace, we should no longer give these episodes of darkness any energy beyond the death we have inflicted upon them by our spiritual sojourning.

The Path of Action

Chapter 8: Forgiveness

The Spiritual Solution- Step 6
Summary: We must honour the cosmic law of justice which permeates all creation. That there is Mercy and Majesty that must emanate from Heaven. There are consequences to all our actions and inaction. Having confessed and offered contrition we must seek forgiveness (step 6) with full sincerity for all that has passed in our lives. We must have Faith that our entreaties and supplications have been heard for ultimately the gift of forgiveness resides with Heaven alone. Yet we can seek to discern signs of such mercy if we are attuned to the insights of our heart.

Forgetfulness is according to Traditional Wisdom one of the core causes of the fall of Man; forgetful of our true primordial nature. Forgetful of the limitless light that shines within our breast.

And forgetful too of the certainty that the cosmic law of justice is embedded within the fabric of the Universe and its order and exquisite balance. How could it be otherwise? A Creator that is Love itself can have only justice and wisdom as the handmaidens to His Act of bringing this world and indeed many worlds into existence.

Too often we may seek to subvert the operation of this cosmic law of justice- that decrees that all our actions have consequences in this realm and the next- when we seek to deify ourselves. And which gives rise within us to that force that seeks to deny the enduring beauty of the Divine Countenance in all we see.

From one who fell into the abyss of hubris (and who honed the skills worthy of the most sophisticated of rhetoricians) easy it became, in my life before my spiritual journey commenced, to act as if the cosmic law would suspend its operations in the world of shadows into which I had plunged.

As said in chapter 2 this "intellectual" sophistication proved to be built on the straw of shallow self-deceit. And now as I entered into the Path of Action and offered my confession and contrition for my failings it was time to stand before the Judge and Justice of Heaven and surrender my heart fully to his Mercy.

"Even if we have sinned a thousand times, a thousand times will the gate of heaven be opened to us. The only condition sought is that we are sincere…"

I placed my hope in the words of Traditional Wisdom which comfort us with the assurance that His Mercy outweighs His Wrath. We must honour the fact that holy Wrath there must be in a world defined by both imperfection and beauty. The Majesty and Might of Heaven must be embraced even if its admonishment is sometimes seemingly harsh. Yet the vision of those that have ascended to the highest of spiritual stations must continue to whisper in our hearts; such saints and wayfarers have assured us of the timeless words written on the Throne of Heaven itself. His Mercy outweighs His Wrath. His Mercy outweighs His Wrath….

Never had these words proved so precious to me. Our role when we seek to return to the path of true authenticity toward our true home (the abode of the Spiritual realm) is to cleanse our heart. Prayer aligned with the sincere confession and contrition outlined in the previous chapter offers us the means to begin that purification within. Patiently we must purify. Patiently we must wait.

"I placed my hope in the words of Traditional Wisdom which comfort us with the assurance that His Mercy outweighs His Wrath."

For Traditional Wisdom had taught me that the gift of forgiveness can ultimately only be born from within the bosom of Heaven.

While we can emulate the Divine emanations through our own acts of forgiveness only Heaven can re align the operation of the cosmic law of justice. Whether we have indeed been fully forgiven can only become clear to us at the end of Time of course. Though we are permitted to search within our hearts and in the subsequent events of our lives to see if we can discern any "signs" of the bestowal of such heavenly forgiveness.

I cleaved too to the memory of the invitation of which I had read which beseeched wayfarers to come and come again to the embrace of the Divine. Even if we have sinned a thousand times, a thousand times will the gate of heaven be opened to us. The only condition sought is that we are sincere enough once again to extinguish the darkness within and walk, however imperfectly, toward the light.

So I began with Faith. Believing that to the extent I could manifest the attribute of Mercy in my own remembrance of the wrongs (perpetrated toward me and by me toward others) in my life, perhaps Heaven too would be so merciful.

In my times with Father Ben O'Rourke (whom I mentioned earlier) we spoke of Divine Forgiveness. The grace and spirit that so clearly animates his wonderful soul helped me to begin this acceptance of who I had been, my recognition that this was no longer who I could choose to be; and that the future orientation of my life would be one where I could manifest the highest within me.

I can visualise us joining together in a prayer of forgiveness which was truly moving and its stirring words are forever etched in my mind. His wisdom left me confident that I could leave the consideration of my confession and contrition in the wisest of hands. Patient waiting was my task as surely the "signs" of heaven would come to release me from the wrongs of the past.
Parallel to this patience I began the important task of honouring the divine within me and offering prayers of forgiveness for those whose actions had blighted my life.

This included family, friends and others who had shared my

life and whose actions, in varying degrees, had dashed expectations and in some cases caused significant and even lasting diminution of the self-love that is so important for us to truly flourish.

Most challenging of all was to come to peace with my late father; a learned man who had unfortunately permitted his soul to become so engulfed in the shadows that even at the end of his life he was unable to bring himself to even look, let alone read, the Holy Scripture which he could recite almost at will. His soul had become so embittered throughout his life that I never saw him display love toward anyone or indeed anything in all the years that we lived under the same roof. His must has been a desolate place within his soul. Choosing to forgive meant a closure that helped heal any shortfalls I experienced in seeking to authentically express my own self-love.

More importantly I prayed ardently for each of the people whose lives I had diminished through the actions to which I had given such vivid confession and contrition. Often accompanied by the tears of regret and shame my heart begged for forgiveness from each and every person.

This included most painfully those who had loved me the most; my mother above all and my siblings whose unfailing support when I had fallen into ruinous moments was always cloaked in the most beautiful expressions of love. More than once, for example, I had become homeless and on each occasion they offered a refuge of love and acceptance which was always a constant mercy.

Radiating out from those closest to me I offered prayers seeking forgiveness from those by whose closeness and intimacy I had been enriched. Those I had failed in variegated ways largely through inadvertence (and, on occasion, through indifference) yet failed nevertheless.

Aligned to the prayers seeking forgiveness was the promise to ensure that such diminution of values would never again become part of my personal philosophy or indeed part of my behaviour in any area of life. No more the insidious self-deceit seeking to justify what my heart always knew was illusory and self-serving. That deceit which can seem innocuous yet serves to always build the next part of the chain we carry around our heart.

Furthermore, I knew that these acts of surrender of my ego, in order to send prayers to others seeking their pardon, would be heard in Heaven given its closeness to and presence within our heart. All the while I knew that remaining steadfast in awaiting Heaven's promise of mercy was important.

"No more the insidious self-deceit seeking to justify what my heart always knew was illusory and self-serving. That deceit which can seem innocuous yet serves to always build the next part of the chain we carry around our heart."

Seeing signs of Heavenly Forgiveness

One of those "signs "of forgiveness I now know, from the perspective afforded by the passage of time, was that the tumult I faced in the collapse of my core business endeavours was a blessing indeed. That event lead to my becoming more attuned to the highest values within me and lead to truly transformative behaviour that de facto extinguished the residual darkness in my soul.

This was the true turning point from an *experiential* point of view in my spiritual journey; this was the fork in the road when I cast aside the "path of least resistance" and it's tempting though utterly chimerical offer of instant escape from the turmoil that I was then facing. Had that turmoil not unfolded my journey would have been much longer; the journey to that highest within me which required full embrace of the 3 steps within the path of action set out above. I know this to be true in my very core of my being.

Over time a number of other "signs" were unveiled that assured me that the Mercy of Heaven was now indeed guiding me; I would like to think this was so in recognition of the sincerity of my desire to reclaim my spiritual chivalry. Three come immediately to mind.

Prosperity of Providence

Within the world of business, I was lead to opportunities and people who helped me to find a path to my true calling in life; something that seemed unthinkable during the business collapse that I have mentioned above.

Prayer's Permanence

Prayer also now truly became a permanent part of my life; this included the liturgical prayers as well as those that could lead me to a path of ceaseless supplication. For such prayers lead us to the guidance so necessary for anyone upon the path to redemption.

Two practices became essential elements of my daily routine. I would a few times each day recite the words "Oh Almighty I thank you" and follow this with the words "Almighty please forgive me". These were two arms of a trinity of short recitals that acted to soothe my soul. The third was the recital of the Divine Name itself. Saying each of these 100 times even once or twice a day literally felt as if my soul was soaring towards heaven and a sense of inner peace permeated my consciousness during these precious times.

I did not always wait for the perfect or most sanctified moment in which to undertake these spiritual recitals. Ideally I whispered them when I could find a glimpse of Mother Nature in what is now almost everywhere the asphalt jungle of modern cities. At other times even in the busiest thoroughfares of London I could secure a sliver of spiritual sustenance from their utterance.

"Prayer also now truly became a permanent part of my life; this included the liturgical prayers as well as those that could lead me to a path of ceaseless supplication."

Personal Blessings

I was also blessed to be "guided" to be re-united with several friends from my youth whom I had not seen for more than two decades. Chance meetings and fortunate coincidences lead to the reunions. Which also included my being lead to meet with several internationally known scholars of spirituality each of whom have made a lasting impact on my journey. Through both their wisdom and their personal example of piety.

Of particular note was the re-union with one former close childhood friend. I discovered that he was also someone deeply immersed in the path of spirituality and indeed had been for many years. Furthermore, it transpired that he also knew very well several of the scholars that I had independently been guided to meet only months earlier.

These astonishing confluences of guiding energy (together with the obvious growing transformation of my heart) convinced me that Mercy was truly abroad in my life; I simply had to look deeply within and around me to see the "signs" through which it was revealing its healing heart.

The Path of Love
Chapter 9: Awakening Authenticity

The Spiritual Solution- Steps 7 and 8
Summary: All Traditional Wisdom speaks of Love as the truly authentic means to return to the Divine in Heaven and within our ourselves. An emotional shattering that broke the vessels of my heart plunged me upon the "path of love". Through that ordeal I learned to always lead with love whilst respecting all other emotions (step 7) so that the world never confused my compassion with weakness. I also rediscovered the courage to always be true to myself and speak that truth no matter what (step 8). This permitted me the peace of being truly self-authentic.

Always deep within the recesses of my soul I knew that one day I would have to surrender. There would come a point of departure from the safety of the shore and honour the imperative to dive into that ocean without a shore.

In the "imaginal realm" there are no safety nets; Traditional Wisdom teaches as we saw in Chapter 5 that we, humanity, stand at an isthmus. Between the Heavenly Realm and the Created Realm. As far as we know we are the only form created in His Form and within us lies the path to that realm where symbols and images speak to us the language of Heaven.

The paths of knowledge and action had led to a profound change within me. The virtual extinguishing of the yearning for the false promises of my own "path of least resistance".

And the aptitude for patient cultivation of the *mode of presence* and orientation that is required for truly lasting change and that ascension into that level of existence which opens our heart to infinity.

To those with whom I spoke about my journey, in my direct conversations and through correspondence, I likened the journey to someone who had been lost deep within a forest of no-thingness utterly disconnected from the Light within and above. My life had become so crowded by the shadows of the trees that scarcely was it within my conscious recollection that there even existed a path to the eternal.

And now after the knowledge gained, a new orientation and philosophy allowed me to lay bare the false gods of the present times even as they proliferated in the iconography of mainstream culture.

"Always deep within the recesses of my soul I knew that one day I would have to surrender. There would come a point of departure from the safety of the shore…."

Further the polishing of the heart had led to an all-encompassing catharsis that had unlocked the power of prayer and spiritual recital into the daily routine of life; indeed, more than this it had shed the shawl of shame and regret and guilt. It had loosened the knots within my heart. This meant that the very lens through which the world within and without was perceived was one forged within the tenets of Traditional Wisdom; that Wisdom which spoke of an ultimate unity of being which cradles the multiplicity we tend to see when we rely only upon our rational faculties.

And yet. My reading had informed me that the true point of no return would require the proverbial leap into the path of love. Discursive understanding of the path of love is enrapturing but tells us nothing of the *modality* through which this path shall reveal itself in our lives. That path where we are able to shoot an arrow of love through the shadows of doubt. So that we can transcend the moment we are experiencing to gain a perspective that changes us forever.

Comfortable in the assumption that there would come a moment when the leap would seem a natural and seamless step in my journey; I (perhaps naively) imagined that this moment may be some years away or could be incrementally realised through supererogatory actions.

Little did I imagine that the path of love would manifest in the form of a catastrophe that I would never have countenanced could befall me.

This took place several years after the commencement of my spiritual journey. A couple of years after the hand of Providence had caused the storm to rage in my business life described in the previous chapter; which itself had of course lead to the intensity required to undertake the polishing of the heart within the path of action.

All my journeying had brought me to what I now understand was to be my true "dark night of the soul"; the one that had been the catalyst for commencing my journey spiritual had shaken me to my foundations. This one shattered those foundations into fragments. It was an emotional collapse that came so close to breaking my will, my soul and the mirror encapsulating my heart.

Entering the Darkest Night

Entrusting a project of the highest importance to another requires the greatest level of trust and confidence in such a person; in my case, this proved to be misplaced and lead to the disintegration of a project (virtually overnight) upon which all my future and the future of those I loved most rested. That the person who perpetrated this calumny was one with whom I had been so close for many years was a shattering blow outweighed only perhaps by the callousness with which the project was destroyed.

My memories of that time are vivid and visceral; the tastes, smells, associative symbols from contemporary music to conversations that took place at the time retain the potency of their effect on me even now. That they persist in the memory is to be expected given the depths of darkness into which I was plunged and the pain that I experienced.

"Little did I imagine that the path of love would manifest in the form of a catastrophe that I would never have countenanced could befall me."

Little is insurmountable to the human will determined enough to see the vision of redemption vividly enough. Yet the passage to that end point can at times seems so overwhelmingly destructive, that the truths to which we hold dear, seem to be eclipsed by the fears within which we become lost.

There is no doubt in my mind that had the emotional shattering that I refer to taken place prior to (or even early within) my spiritual journey it is likely I would have never have recovered. That version of me would have responded with all the emotions of "majesty" not mercy, been overwhelmed by inertia and perhaps even plunged into helplessness. Certainly that version of myself would have embraced the "path of least resistance" (and all the addictive destructive behaviours associated with my version of that path) with more rigour and ardour than I had shown even in the most shadow filled periods of my earlier life.

"Unable to sleep, lost in seeking to understand how I was facing such a catastrophe I recall driving one day and simply losing control of my emotions and bursting into a torrent of tears."

That would have been the frame within which I would have sought to respond to the anguish that this "dark night of the soul" brought to my sense of the present and future. A future that seemed to promise to be one of barrenness and distance from the centre of my life as I knew it. I saw only visions of my Light within being condemned to exist in a permanent winter.

Unable to sleep, lost in seeking to understand how I was facing such a catastrophe I recall driving one day and simply losing control of my emotions and bursting into a torrent of tears. For what seemed like an eternity, I sat in my car at the side of one of the busiest roads in London and sobbed uncontrollably. Only the ability to dial my closest friend and speak with him saved me from languishing there for the rest of the day.

I thought I would need medical intervention to cope with the emotional turmoil within and made the appointment to see my family doctor but I was too self-conscious to attend and cancelled.

Destiny however had another test for me to cope with during this dark night of the soul.

Literally a few days later, as I struggled to come to terms with shattering referred to above, I stood witness to my wife having a stroke in our home one Sunday morning. Fortunately, the hospital stroke team were swift in their intervention-albeit they were left in no uncertainty that only the very best treatment and care would be tolerated- and on the surface at least my wife lost the symptoms of stroke in just days and without any seeming effect on her faculties at all. A later MRI Scan, however, revealed an inoperable clot in her neck which meant many months of specialist medication and during that period the risk of a reoccurrence of the stroke was substantially high.

The ensuing period of months would have been profoundly challenging given only the stroke my wife had endured and the threat of reoccurrence that hung over her and the entire family throughout each day over the next few months.

That this was combined with the consequences of the "darkest night of the soul" lead to the closest of my friends – each of whom I had known for decades- seriously concerned about my mental wellbeing and ability to "keep it together". I think I was placed on a "well-being" watch by them as they checked in with me several times each day.

Perspective is one of the gifts of the unfolding of time. This affords me a vision of this personal "dark night of the soul" as one that acted as a "sign" of the very greatest profundity within my spiritual journey. If Heaven is always speaking with us, as the Ontology and Metaphysics of Traditional Wisdom clearly asserts, then somehow we must accommodate both feast and famine as "signs" that are part of the unfolding of the ultimate purpose of Infinite Intelligence. To think otherwise and bemoan that which we perceive as unwelcome is to usurp the role of Creator and think we can control that which lies beyond our limited (though abundant) faculties.

For it was at this moment, more than anything else that had come to pass in my spiritual journey, that I was tested to see whether I had the strength and courage to be truly vulnerable and enter the path of love. It is said of course that we who know ourselves know Heaven itself. Perhaps this darkness was the one that would finally unveil the full brightness of the light within; which I had hidden and barely acknowledged for so long?

Given my age, the incremental even comfortably inexorable switch to the path of love I had been anticipating, was perhaps simply not an option for me. For tomorrow is promised to no one. We each have only so many allotted to us until we must pass through the door to the next realm.

So I can now see the shattering effect of the "dark night of the soul" was the gift of Heaven's "measuring out" in respect of which I had been patiently waiting.

For surely the pain that others had suffered through my dance with the devil earlier in my life had to be weighed in the scales of cosmic justice. All I can say with all sincerity and certitude (and after the deepest reflection) is that mine has been the bounty of Divine Graciousness such that I know His Mercy outweighs His Wrath.

The Grace of this dark night was not confined to the realisation that not only could my dark night have been far more prolonged and severe; but the recognition that, notwithstanding its shattering effect, had it taken place any earlier in my life it would likely have permanently reversed my ardent desire to transform my life. That would then likely have led to a "hell" here on earth which would have ended in the permanent enslavement and destruction of my heart.

Pain propels the opening of my heart

Now the Grace of Heaven not only afforded me its Mercy but simultaneously it accelerated profoundly my embrace of the path of love.

In order to confront "the dark night" and the bleakest of bleak futures which it seemed to present as certainties, I had to surrender my heart totally and completely; to the love of the Divine and the love that ceaselessly flows and which is fulsomely renewed within our heart.

"For it was now…that I was tested to see whether I had the strength and courage to be truly vulnerable and enter the path of love."

Utterly uncertain whether there could be any reversal in my misfortune (absence a miracle) and the unforgiving future that beckoned I still chose to fully embrace the steps on the path of love. The first two of these are set out below and the final two steps covered in the following chapter.

For it is when we access and seek to manifest that which is highest within us (even where the odds seem almost absolutely to guarantee that this will not avert the pain we must face) that we truly understand that love is, as the poets say, drinking without quenching.

Spiritual Solution Step 7: *Leading with love while respecting all other emotions*

We who claim that we are transformed and further claim that love is the sine qua non of our humanity must demonstrate this in our actions even amidst the most trying of times.

We must have the courage to declare that the vacuous portrayals of love that dominate our current inverted times are the products of the nakedness of the "kings" that seek to promote such portrayals.

For today so much time is invested in seeking to define love- as if we can confine its essence to the categories of our minds- and we hear terms such as "true love", "unconditional love" and other such combinations. As if such tautologies could capture an essence of that which is eternal and embedded within every atom of existence. We live in an age where love is a name virtually without a reality when once surely it was a reality without the need for such names.

No. Love is its own referent. A totality which is simple and which renders it incapable of being divided.

Love demands everything of us. At all times and in all circumstances. Without any qualification. Should we depart from these conditions then something other than love has become our reality.

Crucial to my transformation from Darkness to Light was the honouring of these truths about love. My leap and surrender began the moment that I truly began to live according to what became step 7 on my journey: *Always lead with love while respecting every other emotion.*

So many are the constituent parts of love that (as we have said above) it has no definition which can be exhausted by human language. What we can assert without fear of contradiction is that it demands the greatest vulnerability of which we are capable; it means that we draw up the bridge to our heart- no matter how many times in the past that our heart may have known pain- and let the world and all its imperfections dance within it.

Such vulnerability demands we reclaim our spiritual chivalry to display that value which is the source of strength in true surrender; Courage. A predicate of which is that we embrace both the light and the dark in life which are redolent of the exquisite balance of the created order.

Specifically, in my journey it meant that I had the courage to permit the floodgates of my heart to open; and let the torrents of love contained within find expression in all that I undertook and inform the intention preceding all my actions. At each juncture and even when confronting the cause or causes that had led to my emotional shattering to *always* have love lead the way.

Never let others confuse our compassion for weakness

Yet we who have surrendered to the Compassionate and despite our surrender remain secure in our remembrance of our true nature, even as we lead with love, we must ensure that the world never confuses our compassion with weakness. For our compassion is a reflection of His Compassion which can never contain weakness.

Recognition and honour is thus afforded, within the matrix of love, to all other emotions that manifest as we confront the watersheds in our life. Frustration, anger, pain, distrust, fear, weakness, indignation, each "signs" to our heart that we must interpret. And which must each be seen as manifestations of our reflection of the Divine propensity for "majesty"; just as compassion, charity, warmth, piety and tenderness manifest our reflection of the Divine propensity for "mercy".

> *"...even as we lead with love, we must ensure that the world never confuses our compassion with weakness."*

The Created Order brings challenge and is the canvass upon which the dark and light must needs join battle for the attention and orientation of our souls. Inevitable then becomes the necessity to give expression to the full panoply of our emotions; each authentic and representing the calling of our soul when we face our moments of truth.

This was a powerful realisation and vital ally in facing the "dark night of the soul" that acted as the trigger to embrace fully the path of love; so many conflicting emotions overcame me almost each day during those stormy months. Yet in my prayers I also re affirmed that come what may, no matter what the pain, the provocation or the propensity to permit the emotions of "Majesty" predominate; always, always, I would *lead* with love.

It was my inner voice (that voice within each of us, that truly reflects our presence on the "isthmus", that bridge between the heavenly and created worlds which we are able to unite in our hearts' language of love) that then added the vital liberating caveat......*while respecting all other emotions.*

No need for self-censure or indeed shame when we expressed anger, pain or even rage. Leading with love, and its requirement of honouring of balance and proportionality, I was at peace that such "negative "emotions would be ones that also honoured the highest within me. We are made in His Form and contain majesty and mercy within us.

For the world is peopled by many who have journeyed so far from the Light – whether through the refusal to look up and within or simply the desire to denigrate even the existence of such Light- that they would seek to punish you not only by the darkness in their hearts but also enclose you in their own self- deception.

Thus so called "negative" emotions are to be honoured as reflections of the Divine attribute of Majesty that finds its expression within the human microcosm; indeed, it is an error to label these expressions as "negative" for without indignation, righteous anger and passionate disapprobation much of the achievement of humanity would have languished simply as ideas or distant aspirations.

"This was the lesson I had to learn; to realise that in our vulnerability, which leading with love requires, we have to have the greatest strength of which the human heart is capable."

So I embraced all emotions that flowered to help me heal; each one a guide on the path of love that now demanded all that my spiritual courage could muster. Time was called on the innumerable instances when discretion had become the slayer of valour.

What was important was that love always cloaked the edges of the emotions of Majesty that I gave full expression to during those months when all seemed to be lost.

Incrementally and incredibly the miracle of alchemy began to effect a healing that I could never have believed possible given the calamity with which I had had to contend. There were those who counselled that rage should win, that the thrust for vengeance should be pursued and that an eye for an eye was a precept apposite to my pain.

Yet I took the path less travelled and I can attest that had I not lead with love my life would have been completely different today. Without that love leading the way the miracle that permitted the profound transformation of my heart would likely have been deferred for many years if not permanently held in abeyance.

This was the lesson I had to learn; to realise that in our vulnerability, which leading with love requires, we have to have the greatest strength of which the human heart is capable. Leading with love while respecting all other emotions (step 7) totally transformed my professional life as well as my personal life. It aided the self-authenticity which is vital to live a life of flourishing.

It is important to recall that each of the ten steps set out in this book are in a dynamic relationship with one another. Each of the three paths interact with one another and through self- reference enrich each other.

The ability to lead with love and respect all other emotions, for example, has a profound impact on step 6, the healing heart of forgiveness. Too often those that have been the victim of those that have treated them in ways that fail to honour their Light can find it a challenge to even forgive themselves for such periods in their journey.

Those of us who have walked such paths of unhealthy self-effacement can find a way out of the woods through the expression of the emotions of "majesty". Such expression acts as a spur to shedding the veils of illusion that may have permitted our acceptance of that which we now see as destructive to our soul. And indeed it was through such expression that I was able to forgive myself for the periods in which I had failed to honour myself.

Spiritual Solution- Step 8: *Always being true to yourself and speaking your truth*

Freeing myself to be able to give full expression to all of my emotions was liberating beyond words. Leading always with love gave me confidence that I was answering the call of Heaven. That call which tasks us with finding the courage to honour the individuality which is our unique relationship to the Eternal.

Within such freedom we (who have let fear dominate us for so long) are also able to finally find the beauty that resides within our heart. In that moment we become the authentic person we have always known exists. The one we see in those moments of aloneness when, even if momentarily, we give expression to the language of our hearts.

Until we embrace who we are, and are true to ourselves, we live in inauthenticity. Such falsehood exacts the heavy ransom of mortgaging our soul to the whims of external factors. And we cannot procure redemption of our soul until we, finally, have the courage to announce who we are. Nowhere is this better manifested than our ability to not only be true to ourselves but to *speak our truth always; no matter what.*

Decades earlier I recall reading the exhortation to "thine own self be true" and how powerfully its call for authenticity had impacted me. Often in the years since I had occasion to come back to those words. They always laid bare the inauthenticity that I had allowed to become so central to my life.

"Until we embrace who we are and are true to ourselves we live in inauthenticity. And we cannot procure redemption of our soul until we, finally, have the courage to announce who we are."

The ability to be true to ourselves bears a dynamic relationship to each of the other ten steps and especially to the three steps within the path of action. Only when we permit truth -without qualification or intellectual slights of hand- to be the measure of our meaning can we gain the treasure of real and lasting healing. Otherwise our change can often be chimerical.

Thus being true to myself meant, when undertaking confession (step 4) and contrition (step 5), stepping back in time and facing the unadorned truth of my actions and indeed the intention which fathered those actions which had lead me to the darkness and pain I experienced. Only such self-authenticity leads to freedom; when there are no more shadows to fear, you can permit the past to step into the light of the present.

Simultaneously being true allowed me to truly see ultimate causes that had led to the numerous sojourns along the "path of least resistance" that were now exposed for my heart to see.

It was in this process of living in my truth that I was able to immerse myself into the ultimate truth that sets us free. For all the protestations of Faith I had expressed over the years the truth was indeed that *fear* had been ubiquitous throughout so much of my adult life.

For many who had known me well prior to the commencement of my spiritual journey this would have seemed a slanderous slight; to the world I had always been characterised as confident, self-assertive and even successful on many measures. Yet it is the self-reflection that dominates our heart that exerts the greatest influence on our sense of worth; no matter the adulation and motifs of significance that may flow from people and places in the outside world.

It was I admit difficult to confront the fact (as I was implementing this step of being true to myself) that in so many areas of my life I had been cowered in fear instead of faith. Only in the acceptance of this truth did the polishing of my heart truly find its completion. Only falling to my knees and seeing the cloak of fear that I had worn for so long permitted catharsis in my heart, sufficient to embrace the path of love, in all its splendour.

So many fears I recognised at so many points in my life. The fear of failure; the fear of rejection and the fear of not being enough. How often had these bearers of false evidence prevented me from taking the next step in so many areas of my life? How many times had I baulked at stepping up and grasping the opportunity that had presented itself? How much had I paid in the price of regret for the crucial turning points when hesitation had triumphed?

Though such contemplation of "what might have been" can often be destructive and draining, if we apply thoughtful reflection and recollection to such inner revelations they can act as guideposts for our future.

Thus it was through such acts, of remembrance of the role of fear, that I helped to heal my sense of self. I cleared the mist that clouded the still pristine light that has always shone in my heart; undimmed by my many failings on the plane of earthly existence. Recognition lead to the realisation that I could choose freedom; from fear, worry, anxiety, hesitation and self- doubt.

"Only falling to my knees and seeing the cloak of fear that I had worn for so long permitted the catharsis in my heart, sufficient to embrace the path of love, in all its splendour."

Being true to myself would not guarantee that all that I desired would come to pass in my life; that would be creating another false deity of our humanity. No. Being true to myself could not guarantee such things but it would act as a shield against the temptation to measure my worth by externals.

For being true must lead to the reaffirmation of the principles of Traditional Wisdom encapsulated in the first three steps in the path of knowledge. Knowing that there is a perfect measuring out of the created order is our guarantee that there can be no "failures" from the perspective of transcendence. Such a philosophy allows us to embrace the paradox that we are required to give a full measure of devotion to all our wishes and desires and yet also find peaceful acceptance that whatever Providence manifests is part of the plan written for us. We must embrace this dualistic dance of light and darkness.

And to repeat. Being true to ourselves also enjoins us to *always speak our truth no matter what the consequences.*

In other words, if we discover the unique melody within our heart it is incumbent upon us to share this music with all those with whom we interact. This is made much easier if we have indeed polished our heart and through forgiveness, prayer and leading with love found the courage to know that we are indeed beautiful and brave.

My subsequent practice of speaking my truth has been a blessing of incalculable value over the most recent stages of my spiritual journey. In all areas of my life the effect has been transformative and deeply empowering.

Within business life being unafraid of speaking our truth will not always be welcomed especially by those who have an interest in the comfort of the status quo; yet my experience within the world of business tells me that authenticity's time has come. In our age of ever greater transparency those who "call it as it is" are the voices that are most sought after by businesses that truly want to grow and prosper and meet the challenges of the current age.

Away from the world of business my personal relationships including with family and long standing friends have been enriched permanently by the candour that characterises being true to oneself.

And it was this call to "always speak your truth" that would lead, completely unexpectedly and still scarcely believable even now, to my writing this book. For the relationship that was most enriched by embracing step 8 was the one with myself.

"We must embrace the dualistic dance of light and darkness."

Casting fear aside I honoured fully for the first time so many of my personal traits that I had, for one reason or another, negligently permitted to slowly lose their lustre over the years. This included the fact that I had to make no apology for my passion for the intellectual and for learning that embraces all areas of knowledge. Perhaps I was a "thinker" or "bookish" and little interested in the cult of personality so dominant in our current culture. Being true to myself meant I simply no longer cared to placate this inverted world's emptiness.

Further I accepted that I am a deeply loving person and someone who still, despite facing more than one disappointment of the heart, believes in loving with the ardour of a poet and the passion of a warrior. Crazily, extravagantly romantic was a persona I no longer needed to "tone down" or seek to nuance. I embraced my identity as a stridently masculine man who also knew that his true completion could only come through being utterly vulnerable when in love.

Suppressed for far too long- responsibility for which must ultimately be mine to bear- I found in that "dark night" the most unexpected vehicle to give full expression to these traits of my personality. And to permit me to fully speak the truth and love in my heart.

Years had seen me decry what I in my ignorance (as I was not speaking from a place of informed opinion) I deemed to be the pettiness of social media and in particular Facebook. Yet during that darkest of dark nights in what can only be described as an act of Divine intervention I was guided (by a set of unique coincidences including the impending launch of my first business book) to finally, albeit initially reluctantly, join the world of Facebook.

Initially I simply tentatively commented on posts of those I knew. However very rapidly I found myself pulled by the forces that had laid dormant within me for so long, to pour my heart into the world through my writing. Without fear. Without the desire to seek approval. Without even the ego requiring affirmation or significance.

Rather "leading with love" and "being true to myself" I let the floodgates open. Often writing with tears flowing I shared the true me with the world and knew that in that act of love that informed my words and the images that I shared, that I was at the very least being authentic if not enlightening.

Over the months that followed my life was transformed in a way that still takes my breath away. I developed friendships with so many kindred spirits who were on similar journeys and who were gracious enough to comment on the words that were flowing from a soul aching to share his love. Through the act of writing I learned that I could find a peace that had for so long been a memory. Only that peace that comes from authenticity can be truly liberating. For it does not seek anything outside of itself.

"...leading with love and "being true to myself" I let the floodgates open. Often writing with tears flowing I shared the true me…"

The cloak of fear that had shrouded so much of the luminosity of my light was gradually cast off; in my subsequent metaphoric nakedness (before so many who were strangers to me) I opened my heart and rejoiced in the freedom that vulnerability brings.

Over time (as I reflected on what appeared to be a culmination of sorts in my spiritual journey) the content of this book became an ever more vivid image in my heart. And now I write these words with such a sense of gratitude for the merciful blessing that flowed into my life; the catalyst being the searing pain of the "dark night" without which I may have (as said before) deferred my entry into the path of love. Sometimes only when we are broken can the humility of surrender truly become our greatest prize.

And a "miracle" did indeed take place; the "dark night" passed and was replaced by a day full of more shining brilliance than I had thought possible only months previously. The project that had been destroyed was revivified rapidly in a manner that promised a future far brighter and more authentic than the original design. My wife also made a full recovery from the stroke that had hit her and the family like a thunderbolt at almost the same time.

My heart became the bearer of the Light as it had never been before at any time of my life. Leading with love was as natural as previously fear had been ubiquitous. Speaking the truth of my heart was akin to being given wings to reach heaven; truth absolutely does set us free. This promise is more than words.

I truly put my past behind me and consigned to the dustbin the old life and its destructive habits which had been my most intimate companions for so long. Several of my dearest and longest standing friends to this day are dumbfounded by the extent of my transformation especially in the discarding of the "paths of least resistance "which had blighted so much of my journey in life.

Such outcomes were manna from heaven yet I did not become viscerally attached to them. Instead I focused on the proverbial journey and not the destination.

I surrendered to the perfection of the Wisdom of Heaven. Knowing as certainly as I have known anything; that wherever the path of love took me, and whatever the challenges and opportunities leading with love and speaking my truth might manifest, such honouring of the Eternal would afford me the rewards that flow from authentic self-love.

The Path of Love
Chapter 10: Letting Light Lead

The Spiritual Solution- steps 9 and 10
Summary: *We are heirs to an endless and bountiful world around us and within. All that we require is present if we can truly see with the eye of our heart. Honouring this through the practice of gratitude (step 9) is a crucial step within the "path of love" for we recognise that even the next breath is something in respect of which we cannot be complacent. In the face of such blessings, and even if we are experiencing our own pain, it is consonant with our true nature to serve others (step 10) for such is, in the most profound sense, the highest act of self-love.*

The Spiritual Solution- Step 9: Honouring abundance and Gratitude

Having opened my heart to allow its light to pour forth and lead all my interactions was truly the key that opened the door permanently to a new way to live; whatever the future held and even if destiny was to conspire to offer even greater challenges in my life I knew that my heart would let me withstand them and even prosper.

For the peace that self-truth afforded was as a protection and shield to the arrows of pain or trial that are but a part of the fabric of this Earthly existence.

The daily practice of prayer was the continued means to ever more ardently opening my heart and living in faith. Trusting the flashes and intuitions that would arise in any moment (without having to temper them by the rational) meant that I could be free to express the symbols I could see during such prayer. And indeed in the remembrance of the Divine that became and has remained a cardinal point within each day.

While formal prayer was and remains critical as a means to ensure that I drench my consciousness with that which is Eternal, it was the additional daily repetition of prayers seeking forgiveness and offering gratitude that opened the door to the next step of the Spiritual solution; that of honouring the abundance which is our Divine heritage even if sometimes the external circumstances of our lives act as veils to this truth.

This 9th step asks us to listen to the whispers of our heart; for it shall inform us that it is incumbent upon us, even for the seemingly small or insignificant blessings, to set aside time each day to offer gratitude with all our sincerity.

So I began by focusing more and more in my silence (and during prayer) on each breath taken. That very breath that is the recreation of the Divine Breath that gave us all existence in pre-eternity. How little time I had given to that rhythm of breath I now realised.
How I had taken each precious breath for granted.

"….it was the additional daily repetition of prayers seeking forgiveness and offering gratitude that opened the door to the next step of the Spiritual solution."

Now I meditated upon Traditional Wisdom's injunction to recall that each cycle of breath comprises the inhalation and exhalation of the life force upon which our earthly bodies depend. Thus each breath comprises two blessings and for each there is surely an imperative to give thanks ceaselessly.

Traditional Wisdom has for millennia guided us to recall the Divine Bounty ceaselessly even in the dreams within which we travel during the night. The great saints were able to leave us clues reiterating how important recollection of the Divine is in each new moment.

So this became and remains a vital part of my daily remembrance; to offer supplication for each breath. Even when carrying out physical chores or walking between meetings to take a moment- perhaps a few minutes- to align my breathing for each step with the remembrance of the Sacred Reality.

We need not wait for the "perfect" moment to sit in repose and stillness to devote all our attention to this practice of gratitude; would that we could do so. Indeed, should we be allowed to perhaps all other endeavours would cease; for the beauty of such remembrance would elevate our heart (even momentarily) to another plane of existence from which we would only reluctantly seek to return. Many "Friends of the One" have sought such refuge in nature, in spiritual retreats and of course in the desert.

Now we who live in the grips of modernity must seek out our exile and return in a milieu often alien to the stillness usually required for communion with the Sacred. Still we must strive to capture as many moments we can muster in order to recall how our very existence is dependent on the Divine breath we have been bequeathed.

A second practice that I found flowed naturally from this remembrance of the bounty of each breath was the meditation on the ephemerality of human and earthly existence. Death. Our inevitable companion in the eternal order of creation.

My very life- its trials and tribulations and its joys and triumphs- was finite. Within the context of the earthly body in which my soul and Light subsists. Yet ever more in our modern world we talk so little of the one certainty of which we can all agree; that one day our breath shall cease. We shall depart from this reality. All those whom we love and for whom we hold a special place in our hearts shall also one day take their leave of this earth.

Death seems to have become marginalised or indeed demonised in our contemporary culture. Ageing, in a physical sense, seems to be derided. So many are the iconic representations we see in our world today exhorting us to keep a grip on the rope of youth; now we can call upon the panoply of our latest medical and scientific armoury and - on the surface certainly-roll back the hands of time. Provided we can devote sufficient resources and endless energy to draw upon the various elixirs of youth we have at our disposal.

Surely it is indeed right that we accept that our lifespans are likely to be longer than previous generations and to continue to honour our bodies and minds and flourish.

Yet as a collectivity and certainly in the advanced

economies we rarely-with some honourable exceptions- see mainstream iconography inviting us to fully engage with the inevitably of our mortality.

Traditional Wisdom sees no prison in death; its cosmology offers a vista of many realms to which our light continues its journey after we have shed the bodily garb we have donned in this earthly life.

Accordingly, I undertook my own dance with death for I saw it as kindred to my heart and as a gatekeeper to my Light. This included, as I have previously shared, regularly spending time in silent contemplation in graveyards.

I listened to the whispers of my heart when it said that I should commune with those that now lay at rest. So I attended graveyards sometimes only for a few minutes (if I was having a frenetic day of business meetings) and sometimes for much lengthier periods. I found these excursions offered me glimpses of peace and perspective which no amount of simple reading about death could offer.

Time was given to reading the inscriptions on the headstones many of which were beautiful and deeply moving to my heart. That those who had departed should be remembered was an important part of the true expression of our humanity. Sometimes the reading was overwhelming especially for those whose earthly life had been all too brief. I offered my own prayers to these "strangers" and sometimes my tears too; such was my yearning to give expression to the emotions that my heart felt on these occasions.

Even today I venture when I can to the small graveyard in the church in the village in which I live; I have become familiar with some of the "residents" there. The times I have spent there with my young daughter, silently reading about and remembering these departed brothers and sisters, have been some of the most precious of my life. Long after I too have taken my leave of this world I pray that my daughter is able to find some solace in the remembrance of these times together.

Even when driving past a cemetery I offer silent prayer acknowledging the souls that reside there and offering a simple prayer of love; for I know that I too am destined to join them one day. I cannot help wondering if I too shall be the recipient of such salutation when I am in that purgatorial realm which is the destiny of all.

Over time I expanded my sense of gratitude to encompass all those whose presence has enriched my life. Family, friends and associates are all here to play their part in our unfolding story. I found that it became natural to share my thanks with them.

Even those with whom distance has developed over the course of life have not been overlooked in my offerings of gratitude; in some cases, I have been able to begin the rebuilding of the connectedness we once knew.

As this practice of gratitude (both through the general prayer of thanks and the practice of honouring the blessings for each breath) had become an indispensable part of my daily life I was able to revisit some of the more painful episodes of my life. Only now with eyes redolent with the richness that honouring abundance affords.

I was able to see even the challenging and painful episodes

with such vision. For Traditional Wisdom teaches that all emanation in the created order is a part of the measuring out of the Divine will and purpose; all is as it is meant to be. And within such manifestation there are signs and lessons for those with eyes to see and a heart purified enough to permit its light to illumine.

Thus I able to discern, within the three "traumatic" episodes to which I have alluded throughout this book, evidence of this Divine measuring out.

- The first (my crisis of meaning) was now seen as the necessary impetus needed to truly undertake the spiritual journey which I now know my heart has always been seeking.
- The second (my business collapse a couple of years later) came at a moment when my journey was proceeding but when the battle with the path of least resistance was raging; that business collapse brought my full focus back to the task of polishing my heart within the path of action.
- Finally, the profound "dark night" which occurred late in 2016 proved to be pivotal in plunging me onto the path of love. That path without which my true and final transformation would likely not have been possible.

Through this re-reading of the language of heaven I was able to give gratitude even for what seemed to be the most challenging times in my life.

"For Traditional Wisdom teaches that all emanation in the created order is a part of the measuring out of the Divine will and purpose; all is as it is meant to be."

On a broader perspective it has made me realise that there should be no cowering or worrying about the uncertainties of the future. Instead when challenge arises my heart tells me to embrace the episode- large or small- as a returning prodigal in whose bosom resides another lesson to discern. In all manifestation of the Majesty and Mercy of heaven there is endless Wisdom if we choose to seek it.

This acceptance and indeed joyous embrace of all that life manifests have afforded me the prize that is perhaps most precious and priceless; peace. I cannot say that I have completely vanquished the doom laden voice of my lower soul when a difficulty arises. But it is now habitually drowned out by the music of my heart's recalling that this is but another step on the ladder of wisdom and surrender.

Through Traditional Wisdom I can now see all times of trial as simply waves on the surface of an ocean. No doubt some leave us awe struck yet our heart knows that their existence is ephemeral. For the light in our hearts represent the very ocean itself. Vast, powerful and life affirming.

And so I have largely been able to eschew panic in favour

of peace. Knowing that in that moment, that always exists between stimulation and response, I can find repose in the strength of knowing we are all made in the Form of the Eternal Principal. And if we were to rediscover only this great truth on our spiritual journeying, surely our sojourns would have been worthwhile.

The Spiritual Solution- Step 10: Serving others

We now come to the final step in the "spiritual solution" that has afforded me the blessing of moving from darkness to light. Once again I did not wait for all the other steps to be completed before I embarked on this final crucial step. The dynamic conversation that exists between each step and within and between each of the three paths of knowledge, action and love is never ceasing.

Serving others is in many senses the "sine qua non" of having a sense of gratitude (or honouring abundance as we described it in step 9 above); for when we serve we sacrifice. Our time, perhaps our resources and certainly a part of our hearts if our desire to serve is truly selfless.

In our service of others, we are implicitly acknowledging the ever abundant renewal of the universe in each moment which is a core tenet of Traditional Wisdom. Our sacrifice is founded on the faith that we are constantly the recipients of a replenishing force of Divine Love that is ceaseless.

When I faced my darkest hour in 2016 (when at times I had difficulty even breathing properly and felt at my very lowest point) it was this step that played a crucial role in my healing. Providence had decreed that, at this most painful of times, some of my friends, members of my family and business colleagues were also facing challenging and transformative times respectively.

It would have been easy, even utterly understandable, for me to have taken a step back and focus only on my desperate desire to journey out of the "dark night" which was threatening each day to engulf me completely.

"In our service of others we are implicitly acknowledging the ever abundant renewal of the universe in each moment…."

Yet the importance of leading with love meant I heard the call of my heart to serve others; to put aside, even temporarily, my own pain in order to serve those that needed me most.

This of course included my wife. The timing of whose stroke was remarkable; it virtually coincided (it happened just a few days later) with the "dark night" descending with crushing force into my life.

Somehow I knew that it was at this moment that my wife needed me most. As she bravely faced such a potentially damaging health challenge. I recall even now with vivid clarity how I was pulled apart by two forces. The first called on all my resources and forthright force to ensure that she met with the very best medical advisors available as soon as possible; and at the same time there was the force within trying to keep the fabric of my soul intact as it tried to make sense of the "dark night" that had befallen it.

Similarly, at this time, a very close friend was experiencing profound challenges in life and was on the brink of a very dangerous despair. Furthermore, one of the key businesses where I play a role as an advisor to the Board was facing a seminal moment in its evolution; a moment that required making some very tough changes with significant commercial, financial and indeed emotional implications for the business as a whole.

As these events unfolded in the initial days and weeks (as said a remarkable "coincidence" in terms of timing- following my "dark night") my heart impelled me to step up to the challenge. To display the courage within in order to serve my friend and my colleagues in business. In the knowledge that my help would be of great value to them at these critical junctures of their own journeys.

Yet there was no sense of overwhelm at having to fracture my sense of self to meet these challenges. This enabled me to be the support needed by my wife, very close friend and business colleagues; and also simultaneously embrace the sense of pain that had to be confronted in order for me to heal and journey to my inner light.

Indeed, I became the beneficiary of a burst of zestful energy such that I was frenetically able to balance all these blessings and their demands on my time and internal resources. In fact, I felt a sense of release and vigour that I had not experienced for many years. Serving others came naturally given the disposition of my heart; the new disposition and orientation which I had cultivated over the years of my spiritual journey began several years earlier.

Nevertheless, more than one friend expressed their concerns that I was perhaps (in their words) "heading for a breakdown". That by seeking to undertake all these responsibilities, while being in so much pain within, would lead to my being overwhelmed physically and emotionally.

I would agree that, the person who I had been, would likely have indeed headed for a breakdown; in fact, that person would have turned to the "paths of least resistance" in the above circumstances. He would have subordinated love to less exalted emotions. Further he would likely not have even given anything more than lip service to the idea of serving others in their time of need when his own need was so great.

That person, however, was no longer part of my present; he had been completely reborn and made anew. With a heart that was full of love. A love that had been present always but which he had for so many fear-lead reasons kept largely hidden and denied it the expression which it so craved.

Indeed, my desire to serve became a driving passion I pursued in all parts of my life.

Within the wider field of my business endeavours, for example, I also met some wonderful new people many of whom have become friends. Always leading with love and seeking to serve, many of them were overwhelmed by my desire to help them with their plans; used as they were to people usually seeking some quid pro quo or deal for any help proffered.

Yet my heart guided me to help where I could; even if there was no immediate or indeed likely to be any commercial return or benefit to me. I had faith that adding value in a selfless way honoured the highest that was within me. No amount of financial or commercial return could ever match the way my reputation for integrity was enhanced through rendering such service.

All of the various ways in which I was offered the opportunity to serve (outlined above) seemed to manifest at the time I needed the healing energy of unconditional giving the most. I know that I was guided and therefore embraced all the events in my external world and the intuitions and messages received within my heart. Each I recognised as a "sign" from the hidden realms communicating their symbolic truths that were helping me give expression to my true nature.

For one of the brightest lessons from this period of my life was the realisation that serving others, with all the love that I could muster from my heart, was the source of great inspiration and fulfilment. All the cache, status and accoutrements that may have come my way from any "success" in my commercial life were rendered utterly insignificant in comparison. Little value, I realised, was captured in the external titles of significance we are enjoined to display for others to admire; such a means to significance and self-worth had always been less than compelling for me but it was now revealed in all its vacuousness.

Whilst any "addiction" is to be approached with caution I can confess that, following the entreaties of my heart to serve others, did become and has remained an obsession for me. A healthy obsession I would like to think!

There was also the impetus to serve others by opening my heart across social media platforms in the months following my darkest of dark nights. Indeed, I had initially been wracked with uncertainty about whether my words would be of any value to others. Yet I surrendered to the impulses within my heart to speak and became merely a scribe recording the insights it brought to me.

Always in the gift of others to determine the merit of any of my comments I knew at least that I was leading with unconditional love. For one of the key traits that I aligned to this final step of serving others was to *check my intention at the door.*

Traditional Wisdom warns that even in the serving of others we can fall foul of the desire and avarice of our lower soul for recognition and adulation. Who cannot have a sense of accomplishment and significance when we are thanked or applauded for acts of service to others? Our actions or words may have helped others who are suffering and this is to be celebrated of course. Yet sometimes there is a fine line between truly selfless service and offering self-serving support to those in need.

"I knew at least that I was leading with unconditional love. For one of the key traits that I aligned to this final step of serving others was to check my intention at the door."

Notwithstanding this I cannot deny that the gracious comments received by so many around the world on Facebook helped immeasurably in healing the pain of my "dark night of the soul". It was through their friendships and the value of my interaction with them that light was poured into a soul formerly so enveloped in the shadows. For that I shall remain eternally grateful to each one of them. They know who they are and each remains precious to my heart.

In any event I avoided any potential danger of hubris and the inflating of my lower ego through the strength of humility which I nurtured in my heart.

For it was through the prayers, that have now become the cardinal points of direction in each and every day, that I found a place to be completely in submission to the Infinite; such "spiritual poverty" or "surrender" provided the freedom to bask in chivalric servitude at the deepest level of my being. Paradoxically when I embraced the fact that I was utterly dependent on the grace of heaven (even for every good intention of mine) this released within me the courage and confidence of a "warrior" in the various roles of my life.

When you joyfully accept that even death is our sibling and we embrace the fact that we may be united with such brethren in the very next moment, the usual fears (of loss, failure and being insufficient) pale into insignificance. For in truth if we can face the certainty of our finiteness on this earthly plain what is there to truly fear?

Honouring abundance (gratitude)adds fuel to the fire of faith. Such gratitude acts to flay our most constricting fears.

In such certainty we can be fulsome in the expression of the love in our hearts when we serve others; our Traditional ontology and anthropology helping to infuse our heart's desire with the values that ensure (as far as possible) that our intentions are pure and honourable.

All of the acts of service together with each of the other steps we have identified lead to the transformation of my life and the healing of someone who had been left almost completely broken and bereft.

And every step (and the demands it has made of me) has thereby been absolutely worth all the effort of the past few years. Few are afforded the chance at true redemption and a return to that precious place of peace within the heart. That I have been able to walk the path of love to that place is a blessing from Heaven itself

PART C: LIVING IN WISDOM
Chapter 11
Trials of Transformation

Summary: *There is true joy when we have transformed our heart to reflect the Divine Light within; such a journey is a reward for those that have been prepared to sacrifice all with true humility. Yet even in times of such joy there are inevitable dangers that shall confront us as we seek to live within Wisdom. Three in particular (tests, forgetfulness and pride) have been present in my journey and only prayer and the remembrance of the price paid in my transformation have managed to extinguish their predatory presence.*

We who travel the path of transformation are forever walking on a knife edge between that which was formerly our reality and that to which we have finally turned. All such change requires all that we are prepared to give within our hearts; it requires that the freedom that we seek is bequeathed when we have given the gift of our soul by way of an offering to Heaven.

Having finally undertaken the path of love I truly felt that freedom of which I had read about. That which resides within and whose fragrance radiates out into the actions and intentions which inform our daily lives.

I have continued to live the 10 steps within the "Spiritual Solution" and this has meant I have felt, at long last, that I have consigned my old life (of being beholden to transience and ephemerality) behind me. It has felt as if my heart has never left the warmth of the Divine Light that has always been shining within me.

Yet Traditional Wisdom carries words of caution to the wayfarer. We who have formerly been acolytes of the world of shadows and darkness cannot expect to be freed easily; from our bondage (self-imposed or otherwise) without that world bringing to bear all of its wiles and wishes to lure us back to that by which we had formerly been consumed.

Indeed, this tension was present right from the commencement of my journey to the light. At times threatening to overwhelm the entreaties of my heart when I was foraging for wisdom in the barren paths of modernism's latest knowledge and texts.

This pull of the world I was seeking to discard was, however, most profound when I had walked through the fire of the "dark night of the soul" in late 2016. That time when I finally opened my heart in total vulnerability upon the entry to the path of love.

"We who travel the path of transformation are forever walking on a knife edge between that which was formerly our reality and that to which we have finally turned"

Accordingly, this chapter is akin to a health warning; you, oh wayfarer, be not hasty in your self-congratulation as you grow in wisdom. Even as you traverse the paths of action and finally of that straight path of love (straight in the sense that love is the shortest distance between the points of pain and plenitude) you must be vigilant of the purity of your heart.

For with a certainty that can be accorded to little else I have shared, I can clearly state that you shall face obstacles and trials and tribulations as you journey to the authenticity of who you truly are. These will come inevitably and they shall be in the form from which you now flee.

In my case the three most prominent impostors to my newly transformed heart played their part even as I surrendered ever more fully to the path of love.

Trials

The first were the appearance of obstacles, from the overwhelming to the relatively trivial, that manifested to wrench me back toward the "path of least resistance"; that path which had been the cause of so much of the pain and darkness in my life. Each of us have a path of least resistance (some of us have more than one of course!) which acts as the dark energy placed in our hearts long ago, to act as an arbiter, of our commitment to the highest of which we are capable.

In the form it had taken for me it had been my almost constant companion for decades. I knew that its slaying would be the sincerest test of the strength of my surrender.

And as I walked the paths of action and love, lo and behold, the path of least resistance manifested in my life (in that form most seductive to me) in such a magnified manner as to be scarcely believable.

Those destructive behaviours which had contributed so much to my darkness were now suddenly calling me again: triggered by the innumerable opportunities to take that form of the path of least resistance that was "destined" for me.

The wider social context in which we live has degenerated so rapidly over the past two decades such that my particular path of least resistance is now openly pursued by so many; where once those who walked it would do all they could to keep it concealed. Now, in the glories of the 21st century, I found the invitations to plunge into the most prosaic of possible opportunities within that path bombarding me with unbelievable fulsomeness.

"Each of us have a path of least resistance which acts as the dark energy placed in our hearts long ago to act as an arbiter of our commitment to the highest of which we are capable."

What I would formerly have only dreamt of being able to consume on my particular path was now offered daily almost as a matter of routine; as one might be offered the most delicious confectionaries in the thoroughfares of the plushest of retail districts.

This was the world of shadows exhorting my return to its embrace; so easy it would have been to succumb.

Fortunately, my *mode of orientation* within my heart was such that it was not so much that I had to battle against the darkness in order to resist receding back into these shadows; but that the *propensity* to do so had all but been extinguished. I could now look such allures in the eye and feel only coldness and pity for the soul that had formerly been a slave to them.

This alone would count as a blessing to give thanks for the rest of my life. My dignity, integrity and self-love had been reinstated into my heart through the paths of knowledge, action and love.

Another "trial" was the appearance of seemingly innocuous incidents that conspired to prevent my taking certain steps that were important to my spiritual transformation. One of the great teachers that I had been blessed enough to meet had forewarned that such impediments would appear in an effort to blow my course away from the straight path to the Light that I sought.

Unexpected family illnesses, unfortunate accidents, unplanned commitments were among the less overwhelming impositions on my time; each making their demands just at the point when I was about to meet an important teacher, attend a crucial gathering or seek to make a special journey of learning.

Even the "dark night of the soul" that occurred in late 2016 came just as I had met an important circle of people whose Light and Wisdom had profoundly impacted my inner transformation.

Again in each case I was able, through the wisdom that I had managed to gain on my journey, to recognise these "trials" for what they were. In that way I was able to almost embrace them as "signs" that my transformation was becoming ever more authentic and lasting. This recognition gave me inner peace, vision and strength to continue on the path of love and crush these cruel conspiracies as they sought to derail my desire to reach truth.

Forgetfulness

One of the most astonishing facts of life is how even after the most challenging of episodes, people who have been accorded a second chance at life seemingly forget the magnitude of such mercy.

I have known those whose very health and indeed physical life was at stake and who (following successful medical intervention) were initially zealous in their commitment to a new healthier way of life; but who, over time, regressed to the very destructive choices that had led to their life threatening illness in the first place.

"Faith is always the most fruitful friend when fighting forgetfulness."

Time can be a great reminder and healer and teacher; it can also, if we fail to be vigilant, act as a thief who by stealth dispossesses us of the memory of the struggle we had to undertake for our victory.

And so in those moments, when complacency may rear its head in my daily life, I seek to trigger the memories of the pain that I have had to overcome. The pain that had plagued me for so many years and which had led to my crisis of faith that had brought me to my knees.

As part of my regular remembrance I recall the "dark night of the soul" and relive the breaking of the vessels of my heart. Far from being "negative" thinking this experiential perspective is rather a refreshing exercise, which liberates me from the encroaches of complacency.

Faith is always the most fruitful friend when fighting forgetfulness.

Pride

Those that have journeyed through their own manifestations of hell (whether externally or internally within their souls) and found the ocean of Love in their hearts are the beneficiaries of the greatest of Heavenly mercies. For reasons that remain part of the Divine Mystery many do not receive such mercy in this earthly lifetime. For those that do, if they have eyes to see, perhaps theirs is a special calling to become alchemists; to transmute what was once opaque within and which now shines so brightly and permit that to become a beacon to those whose purgatorial pain has only just begun?

Whatever the answer to that Mystery (and Heaven knows best) surely it must be an incontrovertible truth that humility and reverential gratitude become the motifs of those who have been able to find their own heaven again here on Earth?

Yet such is the cosmic battle that rages – in the conflicts we see across Time and space but especially in the conflicts that are a necessary part of our sacred psychology- that the forces of falsehood can threaten even the purest of hearts.

Traditional Wisdom speaks of the greatest of sacred conflicts being those that we undertake each day; when we pit the purity of our intentions against the perennial demands of our lower soul.

One of those demands is the lower soul's need for significance and adulation and status and esteem. As a measure of worth perhaps never has such adulterated coinage ever been in greater currency than it today's shallow world? Where we see the brazen pursuit of fame, fortune, and favour now ubiquitous in our media and amongst many of our cultural icons.

As I shared my story of my spiritual journey with dear friends (and indeed with business contacts and acquaintances) I was gratified to receive so much sincere interest from them in respect of it. Further I was fortunate that so many were gracious enough to give me much praise for the steps I had undertaken.

The lower soul that I had permitted to gorge so freely on false fruits for so long also found grist for its mill in these words of approbation. At times that soul sought to inflate its presence with the pride that can easily arise when we mistakenly view our accomplishments as being authored only by ourselves.

Many have been the cases of those whose soaking up of such adoration can lead them, in the most profound journey of the soul, to become "holier than thou" and drain the grace that has in reality been their only true catalyst to freedom.

"Yet such is the cosmic battle that rages……that the forces of falsehood can threaten even the purest of hearts."

Fortunately, recognition is half the battle we wage within; and seeing the guile of the ego and lower soul was made far easier given the "spiritual poverty" that I had begun to inculcate within my heart. When one has been left crushed and realises that only the grace of the heavenly realm can ultimately act as a true catalyst of change and transformation, then clothing our heart in the "rags" of a humble servant is liberating.

For in that vulnerability and surrender of the heart we find the greatest strength; we who do not *need* more than the basic amenities of life (though Heaven may afford us riches for our earthly endeavours) can never truly become fearful of "losing" that which we do not crave.

It was with this recognition that I was able to ensure that even the faintest glimmer of the lamp of pride was met with the blinding light of humility from within my heart.

The one countervailing (and awesome) power that has acted as the greatest antidote to any of the above three forces (trials, forgetfulness and false pride) has been the central place prayer now holds in my life.

The regular prayers and supplications to the Infinite throughout each day take but a few minutes but act as a shield to the forces of the lower soul within (and the forces of darkness without) that can act so destructively in our lives.

The prayers and supplications also act as a sword of wisdom with which we can see (through our heart and its intuitions) that which is wholesome and empowering from that which is demeaning and draining. This sword of prayerful wisdom helps us to strike at the very heart of the offerings and allures of any of the numerous false deities on offer in our modern world.

Chapter 12
Faith in our Future

Summary: So many have been the blessings to a once lost soul upon the journey along the paths of knowledge, action and love that each moment as a transformed soul is a profound blessing. Such transformation is open to all who open their hearts to Traditional Wisdom and sincerely seek its sustenance. We stand at a critical moment in our world; where the battle for the souls of each of us and that of our world rages. Between the "fundamentalisms" of politics, scientism and religion and those seeking reclamation of the heart of humanity and heaven's wisdom. Each one of us can help heal our world through each step we take to return to our true nature as Lights of the World.

All farewells are tinged with sorrow and in this final chapter, it is with some sadness, that I cease the meditation that has been this writing; trusting that you, the reader, will have intuited that my words spring from the heart of one who has been lonely and lost and whose mercy came in the form of a "dark night" that acted as a guide to freedom. And, ultimately, lead him to Love.

The three paths of *knowledge* and *action* and *love* are open to all who believe in the purity of the intention behind my description of them as they manifested in my life and my journey. All that I desire is that they can afford you some of the benefits that have accrued and continue to accrue in my life as a result of remaining on these paths each day.

"From that foundation of Traditional wisdom we can begin in earnest that journey of transformation that can make you see with the eyes of the heart. "

As a brief recollection it is worth recalling that predicate upon which the 10 steps are based. This is the light of Traditional Wisdom. That treasury of light which offers a cosmology, ontology and anthropology entirely liberating from the dead matter that forms the basis of modernism's understanding and knowledge of these three vital grounds for existence.

The ten steps and three paths

From that foundation of Traditional wisdom, we can begin in earnest that journey of transformation that can make you see with the eyes of the heart. Thereafter to live in that wisdom which acts as both an antidote to the continual assaults of modernism and as an inspiration to ascend to our higher and true selves. Once again briefly that journey involves:

1. The Path of knowledge
    - Step 1: Look up and see the manifold emanation of the One in all realms
    - Step 2: look around and see the "signs" of

    the Divine in all of creation
    - Step 3: look within and find the Light of heaven in your heart
2. The path of action
    - Step 4: offer witness to the course of your life with full authenticity
    - Step 5: embrace contrition for all that you manifested which was inauthentic
    - Step 6: seek forgiveness as the treasure of healing

3. The path of love
    - Step 7: lead with love always whilst respecting all other emotions
    - Step 8: be true to yourself and always speak your truth
    - Step 9: honour the abundance of even each breath through gratitude
    - Step 10: serve others as a balm to your pain and as the highest form of self-love

Blessings

Through taking these steps we can all truly live the wisdom that is our spiritual heritage. When we cleanse our heart and let the Light lead we can find peace; that sense of equanimity that provides both comfort in our ease and power in our times of trial.

For we remain capable of angel-ship through our ability to read the language of heaven in the Imaginal World; always remembering that we also remain capable of descending into the hell of our darkness within.

Through wisdom and ultimately love we can bridge the chasm between these polarities. And ultimately journey to that summit where our ascension is met with the grace of the Infinite. There we can reside even during our time within the finite created realm; for we may take this journey to the centre of our being each day. Provided our heart is pure enough and our will indomitable, perhaps we can unite with the Being from which *all* that is owes its existence.

"I have also been able to find joy in opening my heart; this opening has let forth the love long languishing latent within."

While I may be very much at the commencement of the true journey to that summit I have been able to *orientate* my *mode of being* toward the Truth. That summit which is the home to which we all yearn in our hearts; for many that yearning remains drowned out by the noise of the nonsense (accurately "no-sense") to which we turn our attention in the daily procession of the transient. Yet it remains a destination that beckons each of us in those moments of silence when we are alone with our heart. Many are the stations to the summit though surely none remain beyond the reach of a heart truly filled with the Light of Heaven.

For I was one of those many chasing non-sense. Yet now I have through striving (whose zealous pursuit continues to grow each day) been able to find who I truly am.

Most importantly I no longer fight in the river of life to prevent the drowning that must come if we see only the waves; my inner peace and self-love derives from the depth of the encounter in my heart with the Divine. Through that encounter, which was truly all encompassing, I have finally been able to see that the waves are simply transitory and that we each contain the ocean of love within ourselves.

As I have shared in the earlier part of the book (in addition to the peace and self-love that the path of knowledge has provided to me) I have also been able to find joy in opening my heart with vulnerability and surrender and in serving others. Without fear and without hesitation; this opening has let forth the love that had long languished latent within.

The ability to lead with love (no matter how challenging the circumstances of life in that moment) has been the ground of more than one "miracle" in my life. It has been the foundation to have the courage to always express my truth no matter what. A treasure whose value is priceless.

Those that have known me for the longest have honoured me in their recognition of the changes in my behaviour and also in the sincerity of my soul that they have witnessed. They too will know of the profundity of transformation I have experienced which has, hardly imaginable a few short years ago, seen the all but total annihilation of the allure of the path(s) of least resistance in whose current I was formerly drowning.

The journey has in addition brought me into contact with so many new and wonderful fellow travellers from across the world on their own mystical journeys; too many to name and they will know who they are.

The same of course must be said of the teachers and scholars whose guidance and grace have illumined my path so profoundly.

"… we become love itself, through casting aside the veils that have formerly hidden our Light."

Embracing the future

For me the next steps in my journey are to ever more fulsomely and openly embrace the path of love onto which I was thrown in late 2016. Casting aside fear and hesitation and the remembrance of the pain of the past, I strive now each day, to give honour to the love that is bursting within my heart. For Love is the most beautiful of the Divine's Self-Manifestation.

We as representatives of Heaven have a unique ability to elevate our existence into one in which we not only speak of love, act in love or think in terms of love; but that we *become* love itself, through casting aside the veils that have formerly hidden our Light.

My studies in the field of spirituality remain firmly in my vision and goals; yet more importantly it is in my daily life that all of the benefits of the ten steps manifest most clearly. For making prayer, supplication and remembrance of the

Divine ever more ubiquitous in my life, *throughout each day*, is the answer; to that yearning that my heart now openly expresses for re-union with its origin in the beauty of the Divine.

That is a long path no doubt. And only through the continued polishing of my heart (and the humility to know that even the next moment is not promised to anyone) can I hope to attain to the next way-station toward that summit I can now see.

"...the path of action- witness, contrition and forgiveness- is the true bridge from where you may be now to the freedom that must come once the path of love becomes your mode of being."

Those of you who have found that the book and the ten steps speak to your heart have the choice to realise the very same benefits that I have briefly elaborated above. This is no citadel of privilege or enclave of the elite. I am one who journeyed from complete nothingness and darkness; and found enough light within to recognise and to accept the continued mercy that emanates from the Infinite.

If you wish to explore the paths of knowledge, action and love I offer my prayers that yours will be a journey of wondrous self-discovery and one that affords you a vision of the beauty of Divine Truth.

If, like me, you have strayed far from the bosom of Traditional wisdom then I would recommend that you may be well served by reading some of the texts which are referred to in Appendix 1 of this book. Whilst the number of books that can be read is effectively endless I have listed those readings that made the most immediate impact on me and lead me to embrace the timeless within Traditional Wisdom.

Whether or not you have the time (or inclination) to undertake these readings what cannot be doubted is that the path of action- witness, contrition and forgiveness- is the true bridge from where you may be now, to the freedom that must come once the path of love becomes your mode of being.

Through the path of action's purifying of the heart not only will the texts of Traditional Wisdom offer you a more profound encounter; even more importantly, perhaps, your heart will begin to shine the Light that resides within you. And it is that light that alone will – if it has the same effect as it did in my life- ensure your sense of self love, authenticity and connectedness to all is immeasurably enriched.

Perhaps one day we shall meet in person. And in that encounter the honour shall be mine to hear from you and learn from your journeying. For it cannot be doubted that we are all each other's guides in this world.

What is at stake: everything

As we approach our conclusion I find joy in my heart recalling the conversations with so many about the search for unity and spirituality. For this is a time of great significance for our world and such a search is of pivotal importance.

Many are the fundamentalisms that are waging war for not only the world and its soul but for dominion of each of us as individual souls within that World Soul.

Most of us have been inundated with images from our media of the seemingly most "obvious" of these fundamentalisms; that of religious fundamentalism. Groups who have given sole sovereignty to the externals of their own Traditions. To the exclusion of the inner paths that lead from the externals of each Tradition to the same centre of all Traditions.

Yet this distortion itself may be a reaction to the second Fundamentalism I have in mind; that of Modernism itself, which seeks to impose- formerly through coercion and now slightly more subtly-its monolithic modes of being. A mode of being which exhorts all to sacrifice upon the altar of Man as Deity; and which seeks to impose this on all peoples, even those whose very different histories do not share modernism's posited conflict between reason and Faith.

The third fundamentalism (surely one of the handmaidens to the birth of modernism as we have defined it) is that of "scientism". That view that sees only that which can be measured as having any reality at all; that which sees only the motion and interaction of fragments of physical matter and energy as being the foundation of any claim to what may be described as truth.

"For this is a time of great significance for our world…...Many are the fundamentalisms that are waging war for not only the world and its soul but for dominion of each of us as individual souls within that World Soul. "

As these three forces play out their battle on a global scale we are entering a period today where the consequent nihilism has given warrant to some of the worst atrocities we have seen for generations; and that is also giving warrant to many leaders who seek to divide and deride. Who see domination and distance as the only means to honour existence.

And it is we, travellers who are searching for that pole of spiritual strength to which all else can cling, who have the opportunity and responsibility to resist these totalitarian claims.

Healing our world

Traditional Wisdom offers a way out of this growing stranglehold; for it offers a far richer view of the realms of existence and most importantly the centrifugal force of the human heart to unite the world where others would have us disintegrate it.

For our actions, intentions and thoughts as individuals are creative forces on a cosmic scale in the sacred cosmology we have reclaimed. Such creative forces that we manifest from our heart and the Light that animates that heart can truly heal. Heal not only our individual souls and the pain we have experienced. But also heal and mend the world and its pain.

We are made uniquely in the image and form of the Infinite and that Light shines within each of us; we refract that Light through our individuated hearts and become the Infinite we are designed to be.

Parting Prayer

I would like to conclude if I may with the words of one of the most wonderful mystic saints of human history; he was also a philosopher, jurist and theologian of the first rank. His works have been of great value to me on my journey. In medieval Europe he was known as Algazel and his words resonate centuries after he wrote them:

"Live as long as you want but know you will one day die

*Love whatever you want but know one day you
will be separated from the object of your love*

*Do whatever you want but know one day you will be
repaid for it"*

It is my firm conviction that all our truth has consequences that reverberate for all time; my parting prayer is that we each have the courage to take the responsibility to make those consequences magnificent.

Amen.

Appendix One - suggested readings

The number of texts and books that I have read throughout my spiritual journey of recent years numbers many hundreds.

Several friends have asked if I could recommend just three books, as a starting point, what would they be: that is a tough question and (cheating a little) I would suggest:

1. Christian, Jewish and Islamic Spirituality volumes
2. The World Turned Inside Out by Tom Cheetham and
3. Four Wise Men by Mark W. Muesse

The above list notwithstanding I would also regard as indispensable "Knowledge and the Sacred" by S H Nasr, "Hidden Treasure" by Fr Ben O'Rourke and "A Return to the Spirit" by Martin Lings. And in respect of the relationship between science and Faith then "The Big Questions in Science and Religion" by Keith Ward is outstanding.

Below I have sought to list a few of the books that have been particularly powerful in addressing my crisis of meaning and restoring the Light of Traditional Wisdom within my heart. I trust they may be of value to you.

Traditional Wisdom and Spirituality

1. Christian Spirituality I, II and III, edited by Bernard McGinn, Crossroad, New York, 1985

2. Jewish Spirituality I and II, edited by Arthur Green, Crossroad, New York, 1985
3. Islamic Spirituality I and II, edited by Seyyed Hossein Nasr, Crossroad, New York, 1985
4. Four Wise Men by Mark W Muesse, Cascade Books, 2017
5. Knowledge and the Sacred by Seyyed Hossein Nasr, SUNY press, 1989
6. The World Turned Inside Out, Tom Cheetham, Spring Journal Books, 2015
7. Finding Your Hidden Treasure by Beningus O'Rourke, Darton, Longman and Todd, 2011
8. Christians, Muslims and Jesus, Mona Siddiqui, Yale University Press, 2014
9. The Case for God, Karen Armstrong, The Bodley Head, 2009
10. Kabbalah: New Perspectives, Moshe Idel, Yale University Press, 1988

Faith and Science

1. The Big Questions in Science and Religion, Keith Ward, Templeton Press, 2008
2. Religion and the Order of Nature by Seyyed Hossein Nasr, OUP, 1996
3. More than Matter, Keith Ward, Lion Hudson, 2010
4. Gunning for God, John C Lennox, Lion Hudson, 2011
5. The New Frontier of Religion and Science, John Hick, Palgrave, 2006
6. Man and Nature, Seyyed Hossein Nasr, ABC International Group, 1997
7. Why God Won't Go Away, Alister McGrath, SPCK, 2011
8. God's Undertaker, John C Lennox, Lion Books, 2009

9. The Language of God, Francis Collins, Simon & Schuster, 2007
10. There is a God, Antony Flew, Harper One, 2008

Suggested Specialist Reading

1. Sufism: A Beginner's Guide, William Chittick, One World, 2007
2. My Soul is a Woman, Annemarie Schimmel, Continuum, 2003
3. Major Trends in Jewish Mysticism, Gershom Scholem, Schocken Books, 1995
4. Essential Writings of Christian Mysticism, Bernard McGinn, Modern Library, 2006
5. Paths to Transcendence, Reza Shah Kazemi, World Wisdom, 2006
6. Confessions, St Augustine, translated by Beningus O'Rourke, Darton, Longman and Todd, 2013
7. Paths to the Heart: Sufism and the Christian East, edited by James S Cutsinger, World Wisdom, 2002
8. An Interpretation of Religion, John Hick, Palgrave, 1989
9. Mystical Union in Judaism, Christianity and Islam, Moshe Idel and Bernard McGinn, Continuum, 1989
10. Mystical Languages of Unsaying, Micheal A Sells, University of Chicago, 1994

As a footnote I have of course consulted and read (with an ever more open heart) many of the sacred (or canonical) texts from the great Faith Traditions of the world ranging from Christianity to Islam and Buddhism to Taoism. Each of the sacred texts by their nature carry the most profound wisdom within them across many levels of meaning.

Appendix Two - The Spiritual Solution

From the foundation of Traditional wisdom (which is set out in chapter 5 ("Reclaiming Wisdom") of the book) we can begin in earnest that journey of transformation. Once again that journey involves these 10 steps:

<u>The Path of Knowledge</u>
- **Step 1**: look up and see the manifold emanation of the One in all realms
- **Step 2**: look around and see the "signs" of the Divine in all of creation
- **Step 3**: look within and find the Light of heaven in your heart

<u>The Path of Action</u>
- **Step 4**: offer witness the course of your life with full authenticity
- **Step 5**: embrace contrition for all that you manifested which was inauthentic
- **Step 6**: seek forgiveness as the treasure of healing

<u>The Path of Love</u>
- **Step 7**: lead with love always whilst respecting all other emotions
- **Step 8**: be true to yourself and always speak your truth
- **Step 9**: honour the abundance of even each breath through gratitude
- **Step 10**: serve others as a balm to your pain and as the highest form of self-love